Great Michigan Deer Tales

Book 4

Great Michigan Deer Tales Book 4

Stories Behind Michigan's Biggest Bucks

Richard P. Smith

Leland Township Library
203 E. Cedar St. Box 736
Leland, MI 49654

Smith Publications

Great Michigan Deer Tales - Book 4
Stories Behind Michigan's Biggest Bucks

by Richard P. Smith

Published by:
    Smith Publications
    Richard P. Smith
    Lucy J. La Faive
    814 Clark St.
    Marquette, MI 49855

All rights reserved. No part of this book may be reproduced or transmitted in any form or any means, electronic or mechanical, including photocopying, recording or by any information storage and retrieval system without written permission from the author, except for the inclusion of brief quotations in a review.

Copyright © 2005 by Richard P. Smith
First Printing 2005
Printed in the United States of America

All photos by the author unless otherwise credited
Cover photo by Richard P. Smith
Back cover design plan by Lucy J. La Faive
Cover and Interior Layout by Globe Printing

Library of Congress Cataloging in Publication Data
Smith, Richard P.
Great Michigan Deer Tales - Book 4: Stories Behind Michigan's Biggest Bucks/ by Richard P. Smith
Deer hunting–Michigan
SK 301.S6 2005 bk.4   799.27SM bk.4
ISBN 0-9710355-1-2 Softcover

FOR BETTY V. ANDREW,
my wonderful mother, who passed away a few days before her 82nd birthday during March of 2005. She always encouraged my interest in the outdoors and writing!

Contents

Chapter 1 - ROMPOLA BUCK REAL — 11

Chapter 2 - WORLD RECORD 8-POINT — 23

Chapter 3 - CASS COUNTY BOW RECORD — 31

Chapter 4 - VAN BUREN COUNTY RECORD — 39

Chapter 5 - HILLSDALE COUNTY'S BEST BUCK — 45

Chapter 6 - 20-POINTER SCORES 220 — 51

Chapter 7 - 16 IS HIS LUCKY NUMBER — 57

Chapter 8 - KEWEENAW COUNTY NONTYPICAL — 63

Chapter 9 - 8-YEAR-OLD BOONER FROM THE U.P. — 69

Chapter 10 - 2002'S BEST TYPICAL — 75

Chapter 11 - THE NEWMAN BUCK — 81

Chapter 12 - SAGINAW COUNTY BOONER — 87

Chapter 13 - MICHIGAN'S HEAVIEST BUCK — 93

Chapter14 - 50 YEARS OF DEER CAMP — 101

Chapter 15 - DOWN TO EARTH
BOWHUNTING EXPERT — 109

About The Author — 125

Books By The Author — 126

Acknowledgments

First and foremost I would like to acknowledge and thank all officers and measurers, past and present, of Commemorative Bucks of Michigan (CBM) for their efforts in measuring many of the big antlered bucks bagged in the state each year and for maintaining a dependable set of records that are becoming an increasingly valuable reference for all big game hunters interested in trying their luck in Michigan. These records help promote the state and give it the credit that's due as a quality whitetail producer. Through the help of CBM, especially Records Coordinator Tira O'Brien, but also measurer John Knevel, I have been able to locate and interview most of the hunters mentioned in this book.

CBM's records are referred to frequently on the pages that follow to help put the size of the racks that are discussed in perspective. How the antlers rank in the county where they were taken and on a statewide basis is mentioned in most, if not all, cases. However, those rankings can change from year-to-year and those that appear in the chapters of this book were current at the time the book was written.

Hunters do not have to have bagged a buck or any other trophy animal that qualifies for state records to belong to CBM. Annual memberships are $25. To join, send a check or money order to CBM, P.O. Box 518, Dryden, MI 48428. For additional information call 810-796-2925 or 800-298-2925 or go to buckfax.com on the internet.

If you have bagged a buck with antlers that might qualify for listing in state records, you should have the rack measured. It doesn't matter what year the deer was killed.

A list of CBM's statewide network of scorers, along with their addresses and telephone numbers, should be available at most DNR offices. Contact the CBM representative nearest you to make an appointment to have your antlers measured. All racks taken during the current season must air dry for 60 days before they can be officially scored. The deadline for each year's scoring period is March 31. There's a nominal charge to enter antlers in state records that meet minimum qualifications, for hunters who do not belong to the organization. Members can enter as many as they wish at no charge.

I also want to publicly thank all of the deer hunters who have shared their tales with me so I could write about them and allowed me the opportunity to photograph their trophy bucks. Extra appreciation goes out to the hunters who have allowed me to use photographs they have provided of their trophy whitetails. I never tire of hearing exciting deer tales, especially those dealing with big bucks, and seeing the trophy animals. An even bigger thanks goes out to family and friends who I have hunted with, sharing deer tales on another level.

My wife Lucy deserves special credit as my partner who published this book as well as took care of many of the other important details and work required to complete this book. Her skill and foresight have made me more efficient in my writing as well as looking after many important business and personal details so I can concentrate on one of my life's most important activities - DEER HUNTING!

Introduction

My wife, Lucy, and I are pleased and proud to bring you this fourth book in a series about what I think are some of Michigan's Greatest Deer Tales. What we're so happy about is that thousands of hunters liked the first three books so much that they've been asking when the next edition was going to be published since Book 3 made it into stores across the state. Over the past year, requests became too numerous to ignore.

Hunters have not only told us that they like the first three books, numerous readers have told us that they have reread the stories multiple times, often when daydreaming about the upcoming seasons. It's a great compliment when readers like the books you publish. It's even more rewarding when they request a book before it's written!

The next time some one asks when Book 4 is going to be published, we will be able to show them a copy of this book. Don't expect Book 5 for at least three years.

Most of the chapters in this book, and the ones that came before it, are about the bucks with the largest antlers known taken by hunters in the state. However, some of the chapters are also devoted to the heaviest and oldest whitetails that have been bagged by hunters. One of the chapters in this volume is about what very well may be the heaviest whitetail ever tagged in Michigan. It's certainly the heaviest that a live weight has been recorded for that I am aware of.

Another chapter is about an Upper Peninsula (U.P.) whitetail that reached the ripe old age of 8 1/2 before it was collected by a hunter. That buck also happened to have a huge set of antlers. One of the chapters in book 3 was about another U.P. buck that attained the same age, but its antlers didn't even qualify for state records. However, there was something else unique about the story behind that deer that made it a great tale worthy of including in this series.

Some deer hunters that excell at collecting book bucks are also the focus of some chapters in this series. Veteran bowhunter John Benedict is featured in the last chapter of this book, for example. He has a knack for arrowing trophy bucks from the ground and he offers some interesting insight into how he does it, so other hunters might follow his example.

The first chapter of this book is devoted to another Michigan bowhunter who consistently takes whopper whitetails - Mitch Rompola from Traverse City. There's new information about a monster typical 12-pointer he arrowed in 1998 that has a rack which outscores all others on record for North America. Two chapters of Book 3 were devoted to the story behind this phenomenal buck and this chapter will add to your knowledge about North America's highest scoring typical. The chapter in this book also delves into the amazing whitetails Mitch has taken with bow and arrow since 1998.

Another chapter in Book 4 that you won't want to miss, is a historical look at one of the U.P.'s traditional deer camps from the perspective of two friends from Mackinaw City who have owned the camp for more than 50 years. The Tahquamenon Club was in existence for 50 years before they bought it. The camp was started by a group of deer hunters from Saginaw.

You can find out about a world record 8-pointer bagged in Michigan, too, along with a lot of other bragging size bucks. I hope you enjoy what's written on the pages that follow!

Photo courtesy Kevin Kreh

Mitch Rompola from Traverse City with the enormous typical 12-point netting 216 5/8 that he arrowed on November 13, 1998. He had no idea the buck would prove to be controversial. It shouldn't have been.

Chapter 1

Rompola Buck Real

The Rompola Buck, a huge 12-point typical that Mitch Rompola of Traverse City bagged with bow and arrow on November 13, 1998, is as real as trophy whitetail bucks get. And you would agree if you could see and hear the 20-minute video I saw and listened to that documents the recovery and validity of this exceptional whitetail. Since the video isn't likely to be available for viewing by the public in the near future, if ever, let me take you through it, so I can share with you the reality of what happened on that day some place in northern Michigan.

Rompola shot the video himself, starting on the ladder stand he arrowed the deer from and then following the blood trail to the fallen buck. He provides commentary along the way. The experience is absolutely awesome as you walk with Rompola along the path this now famous buck took to the point where it fell.

I relived the powerful moment that Mitch first saw the special buck where it fell, stopping to zoom in on it to confirm it was dead before making the final approach to the carcass. Since the video documents the moment Rompola reached the fallen whitetail, there's no way he could have altered the deer's antlers. More importantly for those skeptics out there, the fallen whitetail is shown from many different angles. There is no evidence of any tampering or alterations. Those antlers are real folks!

Besides the 20 minute video tape Mitch Rompola took to

Great Michigan Deer Tales - Book 4

Kevin Kreh and his family saw the monster buck Rompola got in 1998 after Mitch transported the carcass in the back of his pickup truck to their house in Manton.

Mitch took this photo of the phenomenal whitetail when it was alive during December of 1997.

authenticate the awesome 12-pointer he bagged with bow and arrow on November 13, 1998, many people saw the deer over a span of three days before he skinned it. One of those people is conservation officer Bill Bailey from the small town of Honor. Bailey was 48 years old when I spoke to him in 2003 and he had recently completed 22 years as an officer.

"Three older cousins who are in their 50s went with me to look at Mitch's deer," Bill said. "I know they were really checking the deer out. If there was anything wrong, they would have seen it.

"I'm convinced the deer and the antlers are real. I've seen them. How can anyone who hasn't seen the deer claim otherwise?"

If the exceptional antlers grown by the Rompola buck were fake and sewn in place, there would have been obvious signs of tampering. Obvious enough that Rompola could not have afforded to risk showing the deer to anyone much less a conservation officer. Nor would he have gone to the lengths he did to video tape the deer's recovery and show the whitetail and its antlers in such detail.

Kevin Kreh from Manton and his family were also privileged to see the Rompola Buck. Kreh and Rompola are good friends and Mitch took the time to bring the buck to Kevin's home after he loaded the deer in the back of his pickup truck. Kreh manufactures synthetic scents under the name Hawgs Limited that Mitch used to help him finally connect on the unique whitetail.

The three people who measured the Rompola Buck, spending hours handling and examining the antlers, also verify their authenticity. One of those people is a Boone and Crockett measurer, one is certified by Pope and Young and the third is a volunteer with the state record keeping organization - Commemorative Bucks of Michigan.

Mitch arrowed the deer at 7:47 a.m. on November 13th. Ten days earlier, he missed a shot at the same buck when his arrow was deflected. Mitch managed to snap a photograph of the buck before he missed it on November 3rd. The bowhunter also photographed the live buck one morning during December of 1997. Rompola first saw the trophy whitetail in September of 1996. He finally got the buck during his third year of hunting it.

After shooting the buck, Mitch sat down in the stand to regain his composure. He heard a crash that he was sure was the buck going down. However, rather than risk jumping the buck on the chance it might not yet be dead, he went home to get his video camera, his deer drag and grab something to eat. He didn't say what time it was when he climbed back into the stand with the video camera.

"The buck was right there by that broken off stub when I shot him," Rompola says as the video rolls. "That's about 12 yards away. He was angling away. I didn't want to take any chances, so I center shot him."

The spot where the monster 12-point was arrowed is on the edge of a clump of evergreen trees in a stand of hardwood trees. The location is on a ridge. Mitch pans the camera downhill to a cattail marsh where the buck was presumably bedded during the night. There's a valley from the marsh leading uphill to the ridge that the buck usually followed, according to Rompola, as it did that morning.

Two smaller bucks preceded the 12 up the same valley by a couple of minutes that morning. The other bucks had 8 and 10-point racks. Mitch had seen the same trio of whitetails the evening before as they headed downhill into the marsh. The smaller bucks were hanging around a scrape and the 12-point chased them off.

"That's the first time I've seen him that aggressive," Mitch commented.

Before climbing down from the stand, Rompola zooms in on the location of an old stand he hunted from previously. I couldn't make out any detail among the evergreen limbs.

Once on the ground, Mitch shows the stand he shot the whitetail from. It's a permanent ladder stand with wooden steps. It's impossible to tell how high the stand is, but the hunter makes it clear it is on private property. However, public land is not far away. Rompola zooms in on a piece of habitat through the trees and says that's where public land begins.

While trying to locate a blood trail from the 12-point, Mitch goes by a scrape where he used to have a stand and zooms in on it with the camera. Bucks had obviously still been visiting the scrape because ground cover was pawed away, revealing bare soil.

Blood sign is soon located and Rompola starts following it. He acknowledges each new spot of blood as he goes, telling the viewer what he sees. Between comments about the blood trail, Mitch offers other narration.

"The arrow stayed in him," he says. "It angled forward into the right shoulder. I was shaking after I shot him.

"He used the same runway that a big 9-point did that I shot a couple of years ago," Rompola comments. "This is a pretty good runway for bucks. They don't usually make very good runways. They usually just filter through areas.

"They like to run this ridge," Mitch added. "It's so wet and thick down there. It's real mucky. They can't hardly walk through there."

As Rompola points the camera into a thick cedar swamp with numerous fallen trees that he is skirting he says, "It is miserable down through there."

While following the blood trail, Mitch comes upon a tree that was recently rubbed by a buck. He zooms in on it and says that buck sign is fresh. Then Rompola spots the buck he's been after for three years.

"Hell, there he is," Mitch says with surprise in his voice as he looks slightly uphill with the camera lens giving a wide angle view. "Oh my God!

"The arrow's still in him. Ya he's dead. My God!"

It's difficult to see the fallen deer on the screen at that point, but Rompola soon puts the camera down to steady it and zooms in on the animal. The buck's large antlers and head soon jump into sharp focus. The whitetail died facing his back trail. I've shot plenty of bucks that died in a similar position.

"I knew he was big," Mitch says when he reaches the fallen deer. "Look how wide he is. He's in the rut. Boy, he's a big one. Holy Crimminny!"

Then Mitch zooms in on the buck's big front hooves. The right one is notched on the inside edge. That characteristic enabled Rompola to monitor the buck's movements via its distinctive tracks.

"He was dead before I left," he commented. "The arrow did its job.

"Look at the tine lengths on that thing! The brow tines are 10, 11 inches apart. The spread's over three feet. I've got a tape measure back at the truck. My arrows are three feet. He's wider than three feet. I'm shakin."

As Mitch mentioned, the arrow is still in the deer. It's angled sharply backward. He pulls the arrow out on camera and shows a closeup of the broadhead. It's an expandable Gold Tip head on a Gold Tip arrow. The head has two fixed blades and two that are expandable. One of the fixed blades is missing and Rompola speculates that it's lodged in the deer's right shoulder.

"Today is Friday the 13th," Mitch said. "It's my lucky day I guess. What a beauty! What a monster! Look at the gray face on him. I wonder how old he is?

"I first seen him in September of 1996. He's at least 5 1/2 or older. I bet he's six or seven.

"Well, he's a good one. Is he beautiful! I've been waiting to tag this deer for a long time."

Mitch is then shown tying his tag to one of the big buck's antlers. After tagging the whitetail, Rompola turns the video camera off and retrieves a 36-inch tape measure from his truck. He says, "I'm back," after turning the camera back on.

He measures his arrow at 35 1/2 inches and determines the rack's outside spread is greater than the lengths of his arrow or tape measure. He speculates the outside spread could be as much as 38 inches. The inside spread is 30 1/2 inches.

"He was that wide when I saw him in 1996," Rompola said. "I shot him with that lucky arrow. My granddaughter touched it and put luck on it. It's my Logan arrow.

"Man-oh-man. I don't know what the lengths of those beams are, but they are long. It's a perfect 12!

"I'm going to have to gut him to make him lighter. Luckily, the two-track ain't too far. Yup; 1998, November 13th!"

At least two antler-rubbed saplings were in view of where the special buck fell and Mitch filmed them.

"He's been all over in here," he said. "He's been living here a long time. It sure is thick down there!"

Mitch estimated that the buck went about 75 yards after he shot it. Another short piece of video tape following the recovery segment was taken on November 15. It shows the unskinned whitetail in the back of Rompola's pickup truck. He says he wants to shoot more video of the buck before skinning and butchering the carcass.

"I had him officially weighed on a certified scale," Rompola said. "He weighed 263 pounds dressed. He weighed over 300 pounds live weight."

By then he had also verified the greatest outside spread of the antlers as 38 inches. The buck was eventually aged at 7 1/2 years.

"A lot of people stopped by last night and the day before to see the buck," Mitch said. "It was crazy around here. I sure hate to take him apart, but I want to get him mounted."

The exceptional 12-pointer that Rompola arrowed on November 13, 1998 is the second typical that the master bowhunter has taken in Michigan with antlers large enough to exceed the minimums for entry in national records maintained by the Boone and Crockett Club. The first one, which was another 12-point, was bagged on November 8, 1985. The antlers from that deer measured 181 7/8 and that rack currently ranks as the state record typical bow kill in records maintained by Commemorative Bucks of Michigan (CBM).

Mitch didn't enter the 12-point from 1985 in Boone and Crockett Records and his plans for the monster from 1998 were the same. That's why he didn't have a problem signing the agreement drafted by a representative of Milo Hanson that prohibits him from entering the deer in national records until, and if, one with larger antlers than Hanson's is entered.

Some people claim that the reason Mitch signed that agreement by a company representing the Hanson buck is there's something shady about the kill. In reality, the agreement simply reinforced his own intentions from the beginning. Beyond that, the agreement Rompola signed eliminated all speculation about his plans for the deer and effectively removed the spotlight from him and his world class whitetail, which is also what he wanted.

This exceptional bowhunter knows what he accomplished on November 13, 1998 and he doesn't feel the need to prove anything to anybody. He tried to share the thrill, excitement and uniqueness of his accomplishment through television, magazine and newspaper interviews soon after he got the deer. Unfortunately, rumors and baseless speculation overshadowed the truth. What's so sad is the same thing could happen to any hunter.

The only thing Mitch does with the most consistency is arrow mature bucks with big racks. The enormous 12-pointer from '98 was reportedly the 21st whitetail he tagged that had antlers large enough to exceed bow and arrow, big game record keeper Pope and Young minimums. Typical antlers have to measure a minimum of 125 to qualify for Pope and Young listing and nontypicals have to score at least 150.

Although the racks from many of the whitetails Mitch has tagged qualify for listing in Pope and Young Records, he has no more interest in having his deer listed in national bowhunting records than those maintained by the Boone and Crockett Club. Since 1998, Rompola has taken more whitetails with antlers that exceed Pope and Young minimums and a number of them have racks that also surpass Boone and Crockett minimums. While many hunters are hung up on the monster 12-point typical Rompola bagged with bow and arrow in Michigan during 1998, the

Mitch bagged this 10-pointer on November 26, 2003 with bow and arrow during gun season. The antlers on this buck grossed 173 7/8 and netted 170 6/8.

Photo courtesy Kevin Kreh

Here's another 10-point Mitch got during the fall of 2004 on October 30th. He shot the buck from a distance of 11 yards and it had a dressed weight of 222 pounds. The antlers from this whitetail score in the low 170s.

hunter has moved on and continues to quietly and consistently add to the impressive list of trophy bucks to his credit.

As Kevin Kreh puts it, "Mitch told me his time is better spent trying to figure out his next animal than worrying about what other people think about him and the deer he's taken."

Mitch continues to share information about deer he's taken with Kreh and other friends. Copies of photographs of the bucks he's bagged are included with hand-written details about the animals.

Each of the last five years, Rompola has bow-bagged a pair of record book caliber bucks from various parts of the state. During the fall of 2001, he accomplished something that I don't think any other hunter has by taking two whitetails with antlers large enough to exceed Boone and Crockett minimums. One of those bucks was a Leelanau County 9-point that grossed 198 5/8 and netted 191 5/8 and the other was a Kalkaska County 10-point that netted 171.

"A farmer in Leelanau County invited Mitch to hunt

the 9-point," Kreh said. "The land owner had videoed the buck and had one shed. Mitch shot the buck at 4:10 p.m. on October 31, 2001 at a distance of nine yards.

"The G2s on the rack from that buck were 15 1/2 and 16 plus inches," Kreh continued. "The inside spread was 28 inches. The shed antler from the right side that was grown in 2000 was found on March 15, 2001, and it scores over 83. The same antler measured just over 81 when Mitch killed the deer.

"The buck had a dressed weight of 194 pounds. The head mount from the buck now hangs in that farmer's house.

"The 10-point that netted 171 was killed at 7:50 a.m. on December 4, 2001 from a ground blind at a distance of 17 yards. That buck had a dressed weight of 211 pounds. Two people saw that buck when it was alive and told Mitch about it. He figured out that it was living 1 1/2 miles from where it was seen and that's where he killed it."

Mitch only arrowed one trophy buck in 1999. He got it on October 28 and the deer was collected on state land in Grand Traverse County. It was a 5 1/2-year-old 9-point that had a dressed weight of 207 pounds. That buck's antlers grossed in the 160s.

Rompola tagged a pair of 10-points during 2000. One that scored in the 140s was arrowed on the morning of November 8, 2000, in the Upper Peninsula's Dickinson County. Two days later, he got the other 10 that scored in the 150s in Grand Traverse County.

In the fall of 2002, Mitch connected on a 160 class 8-point in Clare County and a 150 class 9-point in Grand Traverse County. The 9 was shot at 10:30 a.m. on October 21, 2002, and it dressed out at 174 pounds. The 8 fell to one of Rompola's arrows at 4:10 p.m. on November 3. The buck had a dressed weight of 246 pounds and the deer's antlers have a 25 1/2-inch spread.

Other hunters had been trying to get that buck for years, according to Kreh. He added that Mitch went down there (Clare County is southeast of Traverse City) for a day and a half and got it.

During the fall of 2003, Rompola arrowed a wide 9-pointer at a distance of about 25 yards on the evening of October 9th from the ground on state land that netted in the 140s. On November 26th of that year, he bagged a 10-point at a distance of eight yards from a ground blind that ended up grossing 173 7/8 and netting 170 6/8.

Even though firearms deer season was open at the time, Rompola was hunting with bow and arrow. He wore an orange hat to conform to hunting regulations.

In 2004, Mitch got a 160-class 8-point on October 27th and a 170-class 10-Point on October 30th. The long-tined 8-point was taken in Leelanau County and dressed out at 177 pounds. The 10 weighed 222 pounds dressed and was taken at a distance of 11 yards. Both bucks were shot from pop-up ground blinds.

For far more information about Mitch's 12-pointer from 1998 refer to Book 3 of Great Michigan Deer Tales. Book 1 of Great Michigan Deer Tales includes a chapter about the 12-point he got in 1985 as well as other big bucks he's bagged with bow and arrow.

Photo courtesy Kevin Kreh

Vic Bulliner with the full mount of his world record 8-point taken in Hillsdale County on November 16, 2001. The massive antlers have a net score of 180 3/8.

Chapter 2

World Record 8-point

When Victor Bulliner of Burton put the crosshairs of his scoped shotgun on the shoulder of a buck with a huge rack in Hillsdale County on November 16, 2001, he had no idea he was about to set a North American record. Nor did he care. All he knew is the buck in front of him was the biggest he had ever seen during his 35 years of whitetail hunting and he was intent on shooting it.

After waiting for at least 15 nerve racking minutes for the exceptional buck to present a killing shot, Bulliner fired and found his way into deer hunting history. Vic killed the highest scoring 8-point known taken with a shotgun anywhere. The rack scores the same as the current world record 8. The deer that grew those antlers was shot with a rifle in South Dakota's Hand County by Vernon Winter during 1965, according to Boone and Crockett Records.

Both of these granddaddy of all 8-points have official net scores of 180 3/8, which is absolutely phenomenal. Darn few 8s have what it takes to meet the B&C minimum of 170 for alltime records. An 8-pointer that has enough bone to net in excess of 180 is definitely in a unique class.

The Boone and Crockett scoring system for typical whitetail antlers was basically designed for racks that have at least 10 points. That's why four circumference measurements are taken between tines on each beam. The fourth circumference is taken at the narrowest point between the third and fourth tines.

On an 8-point rack, the fourth point is the beam tip. To make that last circumference measurement on 8-pointers uniform, it is taken halfway between the third tine and the beam tip. Those numbers normally end up being smaller than they would be on beams with at least 5 points. Reduced potential for circumference totals and fewer tines are the primary reasons why there are so few 8-points in B&C records.

That's also what makes the Bulliner Buck so exceptional. Although the rack netted just over 180, it grossed an amazing 185 1/8, according to Commemorative Bucks of Michigan (CBM), the state's big game record keeper. Regardless of the number of points, it would be tough to miss seeing such a giant rack on the head of any whitetail. Fortunately, what the buck looked like on the hoof was captured on video by a bowhunter who saw the deer days before the 2001 gun season began. After Bulliner bagged the buck, the archer was kind enough to present him with a copy of the video.

Randy Hukill from Midland is the archer who captured some video of the world record 8-point. He said he filmed the buck about five days before Vic shot the deer approximately a half mile from where it was killed. In fact, Randy's brother Brent from Brooklyn also saw the buck later that same day and almost got a bow shot at the whitetail.

Neither of the hunters had seen the buck before that day in November. Randy was in a tree stand by daylight that morning, hoping to get a shot at a decent whitetail, but he wasn't after a specific deer. He had a video camera with him as well as his bow and arrows.

"When I see a deer, I start filming with the video camera first," Randy said. "This helps keep me from shooting young bucks. That morning, I saw movement that I thought was a deer, so I blew into a grunt call I had with me.

Soon afterward, this big 8-point shows up. I thought he was coming in response to the call, but as it turned out, he hadn't heard the call at all. He was chasing a doe. What went through my mind is, "This is a shooter!" That's why the video was brief.

"Other than getting the video of the deer, that morning proved to be frustrating. The closest the buck came to me was about 100 yards. The trophy whitetail went in the middle of a field and bedded down. He bedded on the highest place in the field. After he laid down, I could only see his antlers.

"The spot where the 8-point was bedded was within 40 yards of a fenceline," Randy continued. "I climbed out of the tree stand and snuck up to the fenceline, hoping that I might be able to get a shot at the buck from there. However, when I got to the fenceline, I couldn't see the deer, so I left.

"I didn't want to leave, but my son was on the Grand Valley State football team and they were playing a game that day. I chose to watch the game, but before I left, I showed the video tape of the buck to my brother and father."

After seeing the video of the impressive whitetail, Brent decided to go back to the area where the buck had been seen that afternoon. Neither of them had a clue what the antlers would score, but they knew it was one they would like to get.

"I was able to sneak in where the buck couldn't see me," Brent said. "I walked the fenceline into the woods. After I got there, I could see the deer at the end of the woods. I think he was servicing three does in that area.

"At first, I stood on the ground by a great big oak tree. But then I decided to move to the edge of the woods due to the wind direction, to reduce the chances he would wind me. If I would have stayed by the big oak, I would have had a real close shot at him. He eventually walked within 10 feet of that tree.

"From where I was when he came by, he was 25 yards away, but there were thick saplings in that area, so I didn't want to risk a shot. I didn't want to wound him. If I had been in a tree, I probably would have taken a shot. The reason I didn't climb a tree is I didn't want to make any noise."

The next time the Hukills saw the buck, Vic had his tag on him. That's when Randy told Vic about the video he had taken of the deer and offered to give him a copy of it.

Considering the Bulliner buck's rank in North America, it should come as no surprise that it is the highest scoring 8-point ever recorded in Michigan. The state's previous number one 8-point is also a B&C qualifier and it is the only other rack with that number of points in state records maintained by CBM to exceed 170. Ray Caswell shot the buck that grew those antlers in Delta County on November 17, 1978. The rack has an official score of 175.

The story about the hunt on which Caswell got his monster 8-point is in Book 1 of <u>Great Michigan Deer Tales</u>.

Although Vic had heard about a big buck being seen in the area where he shot the giant 8, he never saw it himself until the day he killed it. Nor was he specifically hunting for a trophy buck. Like so many deer hunters across North America, he was hoping to fill his tag with a respectable buck. Luck played a prominent role in allowing him to tag the exceptional whitetail.

"I was just in the right spot at the right time," Bulliner commented. "I said a prayer asking that we have a nice, safe hunt whether or not we get a deer. I told my son Chad about saying the prayer after I got the 8-point. Chad said the same prayer the next day and he got a 9-pointer with my shotgun."

There's either something about the prayer or the shotgun or perhaps both, that worked in the Bulliner family's favor during the fall of 2001.

Vic said he's shot bucks with more points than the one he got during 2001, but the massive 8-point is by far his biggest rack during his many years of deer hunting. It was the sixth antlered whitetail he has taken during those years. His next biggest buck was a 14-pointer he got during the fall of 1986 on a drive.

"I was one of the standers," Bulliner said, "and the buck came out of a swale I was watching. The deer must have thought I was a tree because he came running right toward me. I shot three times and he dropped seven yards from me.

"The Winchester shotgun I was hunting with at the time was loaded with a slug, a load of double 00 buckshot and another slug. I missed with the first shot, but connected with the buckshot and the last slug. That deer was so close, it's a good thing I didn't have a scope on that shotgun.

Bulliner got that deer in Hillsdale County, but from a different property than where he took the big 8. That 14-point only scored in the low 120s, according to Vic, due to a lot of deductions. He said the rack has a typical 10-point frame with 4 stickers.

One of the other bucks to Vic's credit was taken on the property where the 8 came from. It was a 6-point tagged during the 2000 muzzleloader season that was also taken on a drive. He was posted near where he shot the 8 when the yearling 6-point came running by 40 yards away. He shot the deer with a Knight .50 caliber disc rifle, using 100 grains of Pyrodex and a 240 grain Barnes XTP bullet.

Vic said he's hunted the 80-acre parcel where he shot the world record buck for about 15 years. The property changed hands during that time. When Bulliner asked the new property owner if he could continue hunting the land he got a "no" because the farmer had cattle that he was concerned about. Vic checked with the owner every year and on the third year, he was given permission to hunt the property again.

Bulliner is obviously extremely grateful that the new owner eventually allowed him to hunt his land. Vic is having a number of replicas of his record rack made and he gave one of them to the land owner.

Opening day of the 2001 season was spent hunting in Jackson County with relatives. The party consisted of his son Chad, son-in-law Jason Mathews and brother-in-law Terry Clay.

Bulliner said he saw a pair of does from his tree stand on the morning of November 15 that he could have shot because he had an antlerless permit, but he decided to wait for a buck. Consequently, his group didn't shoot anything on opening day. Jason shot a doe in Jackson County on the morning of the 16th and then went home.

After Jason headed for home, the remaining threesome did some drives on state land in Hillsdale County without any success. Chad and Terry decided to go back to Jackson County after that while Vic went to the farm in Hillsdale County where he had permission to hunt.

"I had a ladder stand in the middle of a swale where I wanted to go, but the wind was wrong for that spot," Bulliner said. "So I brought a folding stool with me that I could sit on. As I was trying to decide where to go, I saw a doe in the swale 20 or 30 yards away. She stood there staring at me. I thought it was kinda strange that she didn't run away. "I thought she might have a buck with her, so I started marching my feet on the ground real hard, letting her know I was leaving. When I was out of her sight, I circled back to a spot where I could see her, if she came out in the open, and sat on my stool. I was hoping she would bring a buck out."

When nothing happened in 20 minutes, Vic was curious if the doe was still there, so he got up for another look. She had moved farther away and that time the hunter's appearance spooked the doe. But he thought that watching the area was still a good idea in case a buck showed up on her trail.

He spotted a leaning willow tree nearby that he decided to climb into. The tree had actually started to fall, but a couple of its large limbs were holding it up. Vic went up the tree trunk about 10 feet to a point where he had a view of the swale where the doe had been and could sit relatively comfortable for a makeshift stand.

An hour and 45 minutes later, Bulliner looked behind him toward the farm house and was surprised to see a big buck 40 yards away. Vic said he didn't expect to see any whitetails in that direction. The deer had to cross a big open field to get to where the hunter saw it.

"I had to lean back to look that way and I didn't have a shot because I didn't clear any branches that way," Bulliner commented.

Vic thought the buck saw him move when he leaned back to look in his direction and the deer was staring at him, so he froze. The whitetail eventually looked in a different direction, but before Bulliner could shift positions, it turned its head back toward him. "I started praying," the hunter said. "I asked for the strength to hold still. My gut was killing me and my left leg was asleep."

After about 15 minutes, the impressive whitetail worked its way around in front of Vic, jumping a little creek, ending up in the swale where the doe had been. To get to that point, the buck crossed several places where Vic had walked before climbing in the willow tree. He credits the fact that he was wearing "scent free" rubber boots for the deer not smelling where he had walked. He was wearing a pair of LaCrosse Burly 1200s that were almost up to his knees.

The previous day, Vic had doe in heat scent pads on the bottom of his boots. Any lingering odor from the scent pads may have also helped to cover his scent or confuse the buck. If the whitetail had detected any human scent where Bulliner had been, it could have spooked or changed directions, eliminating his chance of getting the deer. Besides the high rubber boots, Vic wore a Browning scent free jacket.

When the buck was in position for a shot, Bulliner slowly brought his scoped Browning 12 gauge to his shoulder. The 3x-9x Bushnell Trophy scope was set on 4 power. The deer's rear was facing Vic when he finally got it in the scope, so he waited for a better shot.

As the whitetail turned broadside, Vic aimed at its left shoulder and fired, dropping it instantly with a Winchester high impact saboted slug from a 3-inch shell. The deer was still moving when it went down, so Bulliner fired three more times to make sure it wouldn't get up. When he finally climbed down to look at his trophy, Vic thought the buck had 20 or 30 points due to the size of the antlers. He had spent most of the time looking at the buck out of the corner of his eye and that's why he didn't have a clear picture of how many points it had.

The buck had a dressed weight of 195 pounds and was aged at 4 1/2 by the DNR. The massive rack was green scored at 180 2/8 and,

World Record 8-Point

at that time, there was speculation that it might challenge the existing high mark among 8-points. CBM convened a panel of three of its measurers, including two who are certified by B&C - Cam Cogsdill from Milford and Bert Metzger of West Bloomfield - on January 16, 2002 to officially measure the Bulliner buck. Tom O'Brien from Dryden was the third measurer and he's also certified by Pope and Young.

The whitetail's 8-point sheds from 2000 and 1999 have been located. The antlers the deer grew during 2000 netted 165 7/8, with an inside spread of 21 5/8 inches, and those from '99, when it was only 2 1/2 years old, taped around 148. The 9-point rack from the buck Chad Bulliner shot with his father's shotgun on November 17 in Jackson County was also measured. It scored 119 3/8, 5 5/8 shy of the 125 minimum for entry of typical gun kills in state records.

Exceptional beam lengths is one reason why the Bulliner Buck scored so high. The right beam was 32 6/8 inches in length and the left measured 32 4/8 inches. The inside spread between the beams was 22 3/8 inches.

The second tines on each antler were at least 13 inches long, too. And the rack has exceptional mass. Three out of the four circumference measurements on each beam exceeded five inches. The final circumference measurement on each antler was more than four inches.

There's a possibility that a mineral supplement - Lucky Buck Powder made by Marvo Mineral Company - may have played a role in the exceptional size of the Bulliner buck's rack. The company owner is the guy who gave Vic permission to hunt the land where the whitetail was shot. He's used the mineral on his property and so have neighboring land owners.

Vic passed up a 6-point on the property during the 2001 December muzzleloader season, thinking it might be a son of the record 8-point he shot. Whether or not that whitetail was related to the one he killed, it was sure to have a much bigger rack the following year.

Bruce Heslet II with the former state record nontypical bow kill taken in Cass County on November 5, 2000. The 23-pointer nets 219 6/8.

Chapter 3

Cass County Bow Record

Bruce Heslet II from Edwardsburg is an extreme example of the benefits of passing up young bucks to allow them to attain trophy status. During the four years he had been bowhunting by the fall of 2000, at the age of 23, he had passed up numerous bucks, including some most archers would have shot, waiting for one that he considered a "wall hanger." The one he wanted finally gave him a shot on November 5, 2000, and he made good on the opportunity.

He ended up with a 23-point nontypical that qualified as a new state record among bow kills in that category, according to Commemorative Bucks of Michigan (CBM). The rack is amazingly symmetrical for a nontypical, with only 5 3/8 inches of deductions. The antlers have a 12-point typical frame and 11 nontypical points that gross 225 1/8 and net 219 6/8.

Not bad for Bruce's first whitetail with bow and arrow. He didn't set out to bag a state record buck, of course. It simply turned out that way and he's glad it did.

The previous number one bow kill for Michigan was a 19-pointer that Paul Kintner from Adrian arrowed in Lenawee County during 1996. That rack netted 211. The story about Kintner's previous state record bow kill can be found in Book 2 of <u>Great Michigan Deer Tales</u>.

Heslet got his record buck in Cass County. That county is not known for producing world class bucks. In fact, Bruce's buck is the first nontypical from the county large enough to qualify for national records maintained by the Boone and Crockett Club. The minimum score to meet that criteria is 195.

The county's highest scoring nontypical prior to 2000, according to CBM, was a 22-pointer measuring 190 that Richard Atkinson collected with a shotgun during the 1987 firearms season. The county produced a booner with typical antlers in 1971 for Ben Williams. That 11-pointer scored 172 5/8. The B&C minimum for typical antlers is 170.

If more hunters pass up antlered whitetails like Bruce Heslet did, more book bucks are destined to come from Cass County in the future.

"I can't count how many bucks I've passed up while bowhunting," Heslet said after getting his record buck. "It's at least 30. I know I passed up at least 12 bucks during the fall of 2000."

Two of the bucks he let go that fall were a young 10-point and an older 9-point after they got done fighting.

"All of these does were standing around watching the bucks like they knew they were going to fight," Bruce said, "and they did. The bucks were fighting for at least three minutes. I watched the bigger 9 roll the smaller 10-pointer down the hill toward me that ended the fight.

"The 10-point ended up only 10 yards from the tree I was in and the 9 was only 5 yards away. I thought they had the potential to be bigger bucks next year, so I let them go."

Bruce was a minimum of 20 feet from the ground in a climbing tree stand when he witnessed that fight. The maple tree he occupied was the same one he was in when he shot his state record buck about 10 days later. He was just inside the edge of a woods where he had a view of a set aside field and there was a creek behind him.

The day after Bruce passed up the pair of bucks that were fighting near his tree stand, he passed up a small 6-point. He was on the ground at the time and made some doe bleats with his deer call. When nothing happened after a few minutes, he walked over a hill and saw a small 6-point coming.

The bowhunter simply stepped into a patch of briars for cover and the buck came within five yards of him. It would have been easy to shoot that whitetail. The fall of 2000 was the first that Bruce wore a Scent Lok Suit and he said it really made a difference.

"I couldn't believe the difference in the amount of deer I was seeing," he said. "I never got winded when I was wearing the Scent Lok Suit."

Although the world class buck Heslet shot on November 5, 2000 was his first deer with bow and arrow, it was the second buck to his credit. He shot his first buck at the age of 16 with a shotgun. He started deer hunting when he was 15, but he didn't give it a serious effort that first year.

By the time Bruce was 16, he was more interested in hunting whitetails. It was November 16 that year when he got his first buck.

"It was windy that day," Heslet remembered. "I walked up on him while he was eating away in a hay field. He was only 10 yards away when I came over a hill and he didn't know I was there. It was a spikehorn.

"After I shot that spike, I decided it was time to start passing deer up. It was easier to do after I had a buck under my belt. I realized there are plenty of does out there for everybody."

The transition to bowhunting was helped along by some of Bruce's friends. Heslet heard accounts from his friends about some of the exciting experiences they had while afield before gun season opened, so he decided to try it and he's glad he did. He found bowhunting for whitetails more relaxing than what he had experienced during gun season. He also saw more deer, had more time to hunt and the weather was nicer than it normally is during the last half of November.

On Bruce's first day of bowhunting, he passed up a buck. It was a button buck, but a buck nonetheless. The outstanding whitetail he shot during the fall of 2000 was at that stage at one point in its life and if it had not survived, Michigan's records would have one less notable entry.

That button buck that Heslet saw on his first day of bowhunting came within three yards of the tree he was in. So he got a good look at the deer and that's how he knew it was a young buck. He watched the whitetail for 20 minutes. That experience, as well as the many more that followed, motivated him to spend more time hunting during archery season.

To prepare for hunting with bow and arrow, Bruce participates in local target shooting leagues as well as 3D shoots. He said he takes his young son, Bruce III, who was 5 years old in 2000, with him to 3D shoots and the boy enjoys them. Heslet took his son hunting with him one day that year and his boy saw a buck before he did. It may have been the nontypical that Bruce eventually got, but he doesn't know for sure because he didn't get a real good look at the deer's antlers.

"The buck my son saw was a shooter," Bruce said. "It had a lot of points. We tried to sneak up on it, but I never got a shot. There were other deer around the buck and they spooked while we were stalking him."

On the day Heslet got his record buck, the morning started out differently than others he had hunted.

"I'm superstitious," Bruce admitted. "When looking up in the sky before daylight, I saw a shooting star. So I wished upon the falling star that I'd get a big buck. I always spook deer in the morning when I'm walking out to my stand. That morning, I didn't spook a thing."

It was about 7:30 a.m. on November 5 when Heslet got his exceptional nontypical buck from the same spot where he witnessed the fight between the 9 and 10-point whitetail. As soon as it got light that morning, he used his Rod Benson adjustable deer call to try to lure a buck to him. He grunted a couple of times and then switched to a doe bleat.

"After I made a few doe bleats, I looked behind me to see if anything was coming from that direction," Bruce said. "When I turned back around, the big buck was coming about 35 yards away. As soon as I saw him, I said to myself, 'That's a shooter!'"

Heslet did what most hunters would do under similar circumstances. He got excited, with a capital E! He kept talking to himself to ease the tension and anticipation.

"Hold still! Hold still," he repeated to himself over and over again. "You gotta calm down...."

The world class buck came within 25 yards and then turned to head back the way he came from.

"When he walked behind a brushpile I drew my bow," Bruce said. "When he came out from behind the brushpile, he just stood there 18 to 20 yards away. I tried to put my sight pin behind his right shoulder, but it was moving all over. When I thought it was on target, I released and my arrow hit him, causing the world's loudest crash.

"He dropped right there with a broken spine, but then he started to drag himself away. I climbed down and put an arrow behind his shoulder to finish him. Then I stood in awe of the buck, feeling good about what I had done."

Bruce said he had no idea the buck had a nontypical rack when he shot it. When he saw the antlers from his tree stand, he knew they had height, width and mass, but he had no idea how many points there were. Nor did he care. He knew it was finally one that he wanted to shoot and he concentrated on doing that.

"After the deer was dead, I got the guy who owns the land where I was hunting," Heslet commented. "He was on me all year because I was passing up a lot of bucks. He was kidding me about shooting a spike, but when he saw the antlers of the buck I shot, he was in awe."

The farmer was more than happy to use his tractor to retrieve Bruce's buck.

"The antlers green scored 215," Heslet said, "and I thought the antlers were going to shrink more. They were panel measured by CBM on January 15. I was very happy that the score went up."

The reason for the difference in score is how the brow tines were measured. There are a pair of nontypical points next to each of the brows and different tines were considered the brow tines when the rack was green scored versus officially measured. Many times when antlers are green scored, measurers will allow for some shrinkage, too, which is another reason why scores arrived at after the 60-day drying period can sometimes be higher than green scores rather than lower.

Taxidermist Mark Freshour of Wallhangers Trophy Taxidermy in Constantine, did a full mount of Bruce's state record buck. He said a poacher almost got the trophy whitetail before Heslet did. While caping the deer, he removed 00 buckshot pellets from the whitetail's neck.

35

Freshour figured the wounds from the buckshot pellets were probably inflicted during October. Fortunately, the poacher was too far from the deer for the shot to be fatal. Unfortunately, there are probably other trophy bucks stolen from hunters in similar poaching incidents in which bucks are killed.

The new state record bow kill was 4 1/2 years old and its estimated dressed weight was 200 pounds.

The deer's antlers had an inside spread of 21 2/8 inches. The right antler was 24 6/8 inches in length and the left was 26 inches long. Tine length wasn't exceptional; there were just a lot of them. The longest tines were a little over nine inches in length. The 11 nontypical points had a total length of 41 6/8 inches. The base of the right antler was 5 3/8 inches in circumference and the left antler measured 5 5/8 inches at the base.

"If I don't get another deer the rest of my life, that's fine," Heslet said. "I know I'll never beat this one."

Bruce may never shoot a bigger buck with bow and arrow, but some one else did. A 20-point nontypical that beat Heslet's buck was arrowed on November 14, 2004 in Hillsdale County by Aaron Davis from Holland. The Davis Buck scored 225 7/8. The story about the new state record nontypical bow buck will be in a future edition of <u>Great Michigan Deer Tales</u>.

Taxidermist Mark Freshour (left) and Bruce Heslet carry the full mount of Bruce's buck from Mark's shop.

Cass County Bow Record

This closeup view of the antlers from the Heslet Buck show how both brow tines branch into a number of points. The beginning of a drop tine is also visible on the left antler.

Richard Peet with the 17-point nontypical he shot with a muzzleloader in Van Buren County during December of 2001. The buck was a state record until it was beat in 2004.

Chapter 4

Van Buren County Record

Van Buren County in the southwestern corner of Michigan really shined in the big buck spotlight during the fall of 2001. Two of the highest scoring bucks for the year in different categories were bagged in that county during different seasons. Charles Felcyn from Paw Paw arrowed Michigan's number one typical bow kill, netting 167 2/8, on November 5th and Richard Peet from Plainwell claimed the year's best nontypical for all seasons with a muzzleloader on December 20th.

The 17-pointer that Peet shot had a gross score of 197 6/8 and netted 192 2/8, according to state record keeper Commemorative Bucks of Michigan (CBM). Richard said a tine that he guessed would have been three or four inches long, had been broken off of the left beam. So the buck originally had 18 points. If the missing projection had remained intact, the final score certainly would have surpassed the 195 minimum for alltime listing in national records maintained by the Boone and Crockett Club.

This Van Buren County nontypical is not only the number one in that category for the year, it was a new state record among muzzleloader kills. The highest scoring nontypical black powder buck on record for the state prior to 2001, according to CBM, is a 20-pointer that Brandon Dirschell of Coldwater shot on the last day of the 1999 muzzleloader season in Branch County. Those antlers grossed 202 3/8 and netted 187 4/8. The story behind the Dirschell

Buck can be found in Book 3 of Great Michigan Deer Tales.

The fall of 2001 marked the second year in a row that an exceptional nontypical was taken from Van Buren County. John Pierson collected a 20-pointer in the county during the 2000 gun season that netted 197 2/8. He scored in a vineyard. Coincidentally, Chuck Felcyn was hunting near a vineyard he operates with his father when he got his exceptional typical with bow and arrow.

Peet's black powder buck ranked as the third highest scoring nontypical for Van Buren County at the time he got it. The number one nontypical for the county is a 29-pointer that Michael DeRosa shot during 1989 when he was 14 years old and on his first deer hunt ever. The 20-pointer Pierson got the year before is second in line for the county.

If lady luck had favored Richard Peet during the early bow season instead of on the muzzleloader hunt, both the number one typical and nontypical bow kills for the year could have come from Van Buren County. He said he had two different chances at what he thinks is the same buck that he later got in December, on the same day during the first week of November while bowhunting. Perhaps the buck still had 18 points then.

Richard said he was in a tree stand when he first saw the trophy buck.

"He came by me 40 to 45 yards away and went in a thicket," Peet said. "Three does then came out of the thicket and the buck followed them. I grunted to the buck to try to get him to come closer. He came toward me a number of times, but was still 40 yards away. I kept grunting and he finally reached a point where he was 30 yards away.

"I decided to take a shot then because I didn't think he was going to get any closer and I was confident of connecting at that distance. I drew my 70 pound pull Buckmasters Jennings Bow when the buck went behind a tree. I put the sight where I wanted the arrow to go and released. My heart sank when the arrow went between his front legs.

"I found out later the aluminum arrow was bent," Richard continued. "That was a surprise because the arrows I was using were brand new. The defective arrow probably cost me that buck. I went out and bought carbon arrows after that happened."

Peet's arrow didn't have an effect on the big buck. The deer basically ignored it. Richard said he watched the whitetail work a number of scrapes and then walk off.

An hour and a half later, after he left his tree stand, the bowhunter walked up to within 20 yards of the same buck, which was distracted by the hormone-induced rut. Richard was preparing for his second bow shot at the whitetail when his neighbor started sighting in his shotgun for the upcoming firearm deer season. The noise spooked the buck and that was the last time Peet saw the deer until December 20.

Although Richard didn't see that deer again while bowhunting, he almost had a shot at a second monster with bow and arrow when hunting 15 miles away the week before gun season was to open. The whopper was 35 yards away and he had two does with him.

"He was bigger than the one I got this year," Peet stated. "His antlers were huge. He had more than 6 points on a side. If I would have gotten that buck, I probably would have quit hunting.

"I passed up a nice 8-pointer while I was waiting for a shot at the bigger buck. The 8-point walked right by my stand toward the big buck with his ears back and the deer I wanted chased him off, but there was no way for me to get a shot due to brush that was in the way."

Richard said he started deer hunting when he was 14 years old and he was 31 when he got his state record buck, so he had 17 years of deer hunting experience under his belt at the time. He's been a successful whitetail hunter, averaging one buck per year. His best buck until 2001 was a 10-point that he guessed would score around 125, which is the minimum for entry of typical gun kills in state records. However, he hadn't had the rack measured yet, so it could score more.

Peet worked at a ski hill, so his job left little time for deer hunting after the early bow season ended. On many days, he worked at the ski hill from daylight to dark. By the time muzzleloader season opened in December, he was able to take enough time to hunt the first two days. He saw a couple of small bucks, but nothing he wanted to shoot.

"When I left work on December 17th, I saw a big monster 8-point in a field. That got me fired up and I hunted the next two days without seeing anything. On the 20th, I climbed in a tripod stand while a buddy of mine made a drive through a nearby thicket.

"It wasn't long before I saw my buddy coming through the thicket. By the time he was halfway through the thicket, nothing had come out. I think the buck knew I was there. When I climbed into the tripod, the sling on my rifle hit the side of the blind, making a loud noise.

"I was beginning to think I wasn't going to see anything when I heard something crashing through the brush. The buck came out of the thicket 50 yards away, made a sharp turn and started heading straight away from me. I put the crosshairs on him and shot. When the smoke cleared, I saw that I rolled him.

"I reloaded the rifle just in case he started to get up. When he didn't, I climbed out of the stand and walked up to the buck. I didn't realize how big his antlers were until I got to him. I knew he was a decent little buck when I shot, but I didn't know he was that big!"

Richard shot the whitetail with a .50 caliber Thompson/Center Hawken loaded with 90 grains of powder and a saboted bullet. The rifle was mounted with a 3X-9X variable scope that he thinks was set on 6 power during the drive. The 17-pointer was his first deer with a muzzleloader.

The buck was aged at 4 1/2 and had a dressed weight of 157 pounds. If Richard's shot with the muzzleloader had missed like the arrow had out of his bow during November, that whitetail probably would have lived to see another fall and his antlers would have grown even larger. However, there are plenty of bucks that do escape hunters every year. That's why the state continues to produce a number of B&C qualifying bucks each year. Some years, as many as a dozen or more whitetails of that caliber are bagged in Michigan.

During the 2004 firearms deer season, another 17-point nontypical with antlers larger than the one grown by the Peet Buck was bagged with a muzzleloader in Michigan, becoming the new state record in that category. Twenty-one-year-old Dustin Hotchkin from Concord got that buck on Thanksgiving Day in Ingham County. The antlers scored 204 1/8, making it the first black powder buck on record for the state that exceeded the minimum of 195 for alltime listing in B&C Records. Look for details about that deer in a future edition of Great Michigan Deer Tales.

Richard Peet with his trophy muzzleloader buck.

Greg McCuiston with Hillsdale County's highest scoring typical and the state's number 2 typical, a 15-pointer scoring 190 5/8. The huge rack has a gross score of 198 7/8.

Chapter 5

Hillsdale County's Best Buck

Greg McCuiston from Quincy had no idea that making a drive for a buddy of his would, in three years time, lead to him bagging his best buck ever that is one of the highest scoring typicals on record for the state, but that's exactly what happened. During the course of the drive, McCuiston stumbled on an island of high ground surrounded by water in a swamp. A couple of things led Greg to realize the island was a perfect refuge for whitetails, so he placed a tree stand where he could intercept deer going to and from the island.

On the evening of November 15, 2001, he shot an impressive 15-pointer from that stand that is the envy of many Michigan deer hunters as well as those from other parts of North America. The typical 14-point frame has a gross score of 198 7/8 and nets 190 5/8, putting it in second place among typicals in state records maintained by Commemorative Bucks of Michigan (CBM). The only typical whitetail rack in state records that's larger is a 16-point that Troy Stephens from Jackson shot in Jackson County during 1996 that nets 198.

The Stephens Buck has a 12-point typical frame with exceptionally long tines and four nontypical points. Although this rack has more deductions than McCuiston's, the gross score was also much higher - 214 3/8. The story behind the Stephens Buck is in Book 2 of Great Michigan Deer Tales.

Greg got his buck in Hillsdale County and its antlers rank as that

45

county's best typical. Amazingly, the rack from McCuiston's buck beat out another whitetail for the honor that was shot a day later from the same county. The antlers from that deer grossed 185 1/8 and netted 180 3/8, but it got more attention than Greg's because it is a state record 8-point and ties for the highest scoring 8-pointer on record for North America. The two bucks were shot 15 miles apart.

Refer to the chapter titled "World Record 8-Point" in this book for details about that deer.

During the drive on which Greg stumbled upon the island in the swamp, he didn't push any deer in front of his partner, but he found a buck that had been shot by some one else and died on the patch of high ground. It was a nice 8-pointer. The buck hadn't been dead long, so the meat was salvagable. When the pair later returned to the island to retrieve the deer, they jumped another whitetail that had sought security there.

By the time deer season opened the following year (1999), McCuiston had a tree stand in place on the edge of the swamp where he could see the island. While bowhunting from that platform during late October, he drew on a trophy 9-pointer that was following a pair of does from the island to a stand of pines, but he never got a clear shot. Greg guessed that buck's antlers would have scored between 125 and 130.

McCuiston got his second look at a book buck from his stand on the edge of the swamp during December of 1999. It was three days before Christmas and he climbed into the stand for some late season bowhunting.

After getting in the stand that day, Greg said he had to blow his nose, so he did so several times, making no effort to be quiet. On the opposite side of the stand from the swamp is a thick stand of pine trees. Soon after blowing his nose, a big buck stuck his head out of the pines 40 yards away.

"There were lots of tines on that buck's rack," McCuiston said, "and they were long, too."

Based on his description, that whitetail had to be a different one than the buck he got during the fall of 2001. They both had lots of points, but Greg didn't think the tines on the deer he shot were as long as those of the buck he saw in December of '99. The buck he

Hillsdale County's Best Buck

killed would have been too young to have a big rack during '99, too.

The buck that showed itself during December may have thought the noise Greg made from the stand was a snorting deer. When the whitetail didn't see any other deer, it disappeared. If Greg would have had a call with him, he might have been able to lure the buck closer instead.

The fall of 2001 was McCuiston's 16th year of deer hunting. He hunts with both archery equipment and firearms. His best buck prior to 2001 was a 10-point that he got with bow and arrow during 1994. Its antlers scored 119. The hunter had also taken a 5-point with bow and arrow and a 3-pointer with a shotgun.

Although McCuiston knew the area held some monster bucks, he didn't see any others after December of 1999, until November 15, 2001. Besides time spent bow hunting during October and November in 2001, Greg put a Cam Tracker up near the stand to try to monitor the movements of local bucks. He captured six or seven bucks on film, with the biggest having 6 and 8-point racks.

He saw a pair of 8s while bow hunting, one that had been photographed by his camera and another that hadn't been. Neither were in position for a bow shot. He could have shot the 6-point one day when it was 10 yards away broadside, but he passed it up to wait for something bigger. Greg also passed up a spikehorn with his bow.

On opening day of firearms season, Greg was in his Strong Built Stand 20 feet from the ground about an hour before daylight. To reduce his odor, he had showered in Scent Away Soap and used a similar deodorant. His hunting clothes had been washed in baking soda and stored in a plastic bag with pine boughs prior to putting them on for the hunt.

After daylight, he saw a doe on the island. A short time later, a big buck stuck his head and neck out of the brush on the island.

McCuiston said he had a newly installed 3-9X Bushnell scope on his 12 gauge Remington 870 and he studied the deer through the crosshairs, considering a shot, but he decided it would be too risky, so he waited. He watched the buck for 15 minutes before it disappeared. It's likely that whitetail was the same one he later shot, but he didn't get a good enough look at the antlers to be sure.

Five minutes after the big buck disappeared, a spikehorn that Greg passed up with his bow came out of the swamp and he let it go again. The spike was the last deer McCuiston saw until noon when he left the stand for lunch. He was back in position at 3:00 p.m.

He didn't see or hear any deer until 5:20 p.m. He heard the whitetails before he saw them. They were splashing through the water in the swamp and he also heard crashing noises as they ran. A doe came running out of the swamp with a buck behind her.

Greg said the buck had a rack, but it was running so fast he couldn't tell how big it was. The speed at which it was running also made a shot impossible. After the buck and doe were gone, McCuiston said he heard more noise coming from the swamp. Then a trailing buck walked into the open 50 yards away.

"I thought it was an 8 or 10 point," Greg said. "As soon as I saw it was a shooter, I concentrated on putting the slug in his vitals. He only went 15 yards after I shot him with a Brenneke Slug before he went down. Then he tried to get up and I shot three more times, but I didn't hit him any of those times.

Greg stayed in his stand until dark and then went to meet a pair of hunting partners that were hunting another area. His buddies were James Osterhout from Taylor and Frank Ratledge of Wyandotte. The three of them went to retrieve Greg's buck together. McCuiston was the first to reach the fallen whitetail and he soon found out the rack was much bigger than he thought.

"I started counting points when I walked up to the buck. I couldn't believe how many points he had."

The whitetail was thought to be 3 1/2 or 4 1/2 years old and had an estimated dressed weight of 200 pounds. Patrick Heinemann of Coldwater mounted the head of Greg's buck for him and he was pleased with the results.

"He did a super job on the mount and also had it back to me by Christmas," McCuiston said. "What a present, huh!"

The fact that the rack had so many typical points - 14 - really helped boost the score. The fourth tine on each antler were over 10 inches in length. Two more tines exceeded 9 inches and another pair of points were more than 8 inches long.

Both of the beams were also long, exceeding 26 inches. The inside spread between the antlers was 18 5/8 inches. The beams weren't real heavy though. Most circumference measurements were between 4 and 5 inches.

One nontypical point was 1 4/8 inches in length, which was a deduction. There were another 6 6/8 inches of deductions for differences in symmetry from one antler to the other.

Greg McCuiston with his Hillsdale County monster where it fell.

Robert Sexton with the 20 point Nontypical that was bedded within 30 yards of him for hours without his knowledge.

Chapter 6

20-Pointer Scores 220

Trophy whitetail bucks probably spend more time watching deer hunters and monitoring their movements than most of us realize. In most cases, we never know the deer were there. Robert Sexton from Watervliet, Michigan is an exception.

He found out unexpectedly that a Boone and Crockett qualifying, 20-point nontypical had been watching him for three hours within easy shotgun range, waiting for him to leave. If it hadn't been for Robert's brother Tom, Robert probably would never have known the big buck was there. And he wouldn't have bagged one of Michigan's highest scoring nontypicals.

The monster Berrien County Booner has a rack that grossed 224 6/8 and netted 220 5/8 as a nontypical, making it the highest scoring nontypical known taken in the state during 2002. The antlers have a 10-point typical frame that grosses 187 2/8. There are 10 nontypical points that total 37 4/8 inches in length.

The rack ranked fifth among nontypical gun kills in Michigan at the time it was taken, according to state record keeper Commemorative Bucks of Michigan (CBM). It would have ranked at least one spot higher if it hadn't been for a broken drop tine on the right antler. Just two more inches of antler would have put Sexton's whopper ahead of a 25-pointer Chuck Scheffner shot in Huron County during 1876 that measured 222 4/8.

51

The buck easily ranks as the number one nontypical from Berrien County. The highest scoring nontypical recorded for the county by CBM prior to 2002 was a 12-pointer scoring 178 6/8 that Dave York shot during the 2000 firearms season. Nontypical whitetail racks only have to score 150 to qualify for a place in CBM records. The minimum is 195 for national records kept by the Boone and Crockett Club.

Sexton is understandably pleased with his buck. It is by far his best, but he's taken some other trophy whitetails over the years. His best buck until last fall was a 11-point that he also had scored after he got the 20-pointer and it measured 148. He got that buck in 1988. The big nontypical was the first set of antlers he has had measured from deer he's shot.

"I'm an avid deer hunter," Sexton said. "I hunt pretty heavy from October 1 (opening day of bow season) through the end of December."

Robert said he started hunting whitetails with firearms, primarily shotguns, at the age of 14 and took up bowhunting a while later. He also hunts with a muzzleloader during the December season. He shot a 5-pointer with his front loader at 30 yards during December of 2002 after missing a 150-yard shot at an 8-point.

His best buck with bow and arrow, at the time, was a 7-point. The rest of his bow kills have been does. While trying to fill an antlerless permit during the late archery season in December of 2002, Robert said he saw a beautiful 12-point. It was with another buck that had 4 points on one antler and a spike on the other side.

It was November 18, 2002 when Robert scored on his book buck, which is the fourth day of gun season. He had gotten a shot at a 10-pointer on opening day with his 12 gauge Remington 1100, but he failed to get that whitetail. Robert and Tom decided to hunt together on the afternoon of the 18th. They went to an apple orchard and split up to take stands until dark.

Robert picked a spot where he felt he had a good view of an area deer might move through during the latter part of the day and leaned against a tree to break his outline. He saw seven deer, but they were all does. Sexton is a smoker and he smoked some cigarettes while he was posted, but he was downwind from where he saw the whitetails and moved slowly when smoking to reduce the chances of being seen. The activity didn't disturb any of the deer he saw.

What Robert didn't know is the big buck was monitoring his every move from its bed a surprisingly short distance away. It was bedded in brown orchard grass that was about three feet high. The reclining whitetail blended in perfectly with its surroundings.

The mature buck had probably avoided hunters before by remaining motionless when approached. The buck may have thought Sexton was going to walk on by and continue out of sight. When the hunter stopped and remained in place, the wise whitetail obviously decided to do the same.

The deer had the advantage. He knew where the hunter was and that the person didn't pose a threat as long Robert didn't know the deer was there. The buck probably planned on staying put until Sexton left his post when shooting light faded.

If it hadn't been for Tom, the buck probably would have lived to see another day and Robert would not have known how close he had been to the buck of a lifetime during his entire vigil. After three hours of sitting, Tom got cold and he decided to join Robert, so they could walk out together. Little did he know how much that decision would impact their deer hunting destinies.

If Tom had taken a different course to reach his brother, the buck might have stayed where he was, but the path Tom took left the deer little choice.

"I saw my brother coming," Robert said. "I watched him walk across a swamp, then I turned away and lit a cigarette. A while later I heard him cuss a couple of times and turned around. The buck was practically on top of me.

"When Tom was walking through the tall grass, he almost stepped on the big buck. The buck was only laying 30 yards from me. It jumped up and came running by me 12 yards away!

"I saw that it was a big deer and I immediately got ready to take a shot. I don't ever pay attention to the rack until afterward. The buck was so close, I simply pointed the gun and shot. I have a scope on my shotgun, but I never would have got him in the scope.

"That buck was moving when he ran by me," Sexton continued. "He was running flat out. I think it's easier to hit deer running flat out."

"When I shot I knew I didn't miss him. I saw him flinch and move a little bit sideways. My brother thought I missed. He said the buck was huge."

Robert commented that Tom was so surprised by the buck's sudden appearance so close to his brother that he never attempted to shoot at the deer.

"We looked for the buck until 8:00 p.m.," Sexton said, "and we couldn't find him. We couldn't find any blood either. We finally decided to give up and come back in the morning. I couldn't sleep much that night.

"It took from daylight until 11:30 the following morning to find the deer," Robert said. "We found a few small spots of blood, but they were few and far between. The buck only went 80 yards, but the grass was so high in that orchard it was hard to see. But once my brother got close to the deer, those antlers were easy to see.

"Tom whistled a couple of times when he found the buck. My brother said, 'He's unbelievable!' The first thing I did is put my tag on him. His neck was 27 1/2 inches around, just a couple of inches short of my waist size."

The reason there wasn't much blood to follow the buck is the slug Sexton shot it with did not exit. Robert recovered the deformed slug from the carcass and it's nailed to the base of the board the buck's head is mounted on.

Interestingly, the buck's dressed weight was almost the same as the net antler score. He weighed 220 pounds. The deer was aged at 4 1/2. The huge rack has 8 points on the right antler and 12 on the left. Three of the tines on the right beam are nontypicals and there are seven nontypical points on the left antler. The right beam is 25 3/8 inches long and the left measures 24 7/8. Inside spread between the beams is 23 1/8 inches.

This story should serve as a perfect example of how sly mature bucks can be at avoiding hunters. Some of them obviously feel at ease even when close to hunters as long as they have the upper hand. When they can pinpoint hunters by sight and/or smell and realize they aren't in immediate danger, they apparently have nerves of steel and don't panic.

20-Pointer Scores 220

This is one case where the whitetail's strategy backfired. However, there are probably numerous times when deer go undetected for every time a hunter lucks out like Robert Sexton did. Many hunters probably don't expect to find big bucks in tall grass or weeds and end up missing out on some prime opportunities because of it.

This view of the right antler from the Sexton Buck shows the broken drop tine on the rack. If that tine hadn't been broken the antlers would rank higher in state records.

Photo Courtesy Steve Williams

Steve Williams when he was 16 with the Boone and Crockett 16-pointer he bagged in a cornfield with a 16 gauge shotgun on November 18, 2000.

Chapter 7

16 Is His Lucky Number

From all appearances, 16 is a lucky number for Steve Williams from Vicksburg. At least it was during the 2000 gun deer season. He was 16 years old at the time and was hunting with a 16 gauge shotgun that he used to bag a 16-point buck that had one of the biggest racks known taken in the state that year.

The antlers from the Kalamazoo County whitetail were big enough to break a 16-year-old record among typicals taken in the county, according to state records maintained by Commemorative Bucks of Michigan (CBM). The rack from Steve's buck had a gross score of 196 7/8 and netted 179. The previous number one typical for the county was an 11-pointer measuring 171 4/8 that Harvey B. Braden shot during the 1984 firearms hunt.

It would have been even more of a coincidence if Steve would have gotten his book buck on November 16. The memorable hunt took place on Saturday, November 18, 2000. Steve and his stepfather, Hal Heuer, started their hunt early that morning. Before the day was over, the young hunter learned a valuable lesson about whitetail hunting in the process of collecting the trophy of a lifetime and that is that big bucks avoid a lot of hunters by hiding in cornfields.

"It had snowed the past couple of days and the snow on Hal's tree stand melted to ice under his feet, making the stand slick," Williams wrote, "so he got down early and came to get me. After a coffee break, we drove to a friend's house to see how many deer they had hanging."

Their friend's name is Jack and he owns 80 acres where Steve and Hal had done some bowhunting earlier in the fall. Jack and another couple - Mike and Lisa - were hunting his property that morning. All three of them had seen a big buck known locally as "Louie." "Big Louie" had been spending much of his time on 120 acres owned by Jack's neighbors, who don't allow hunting, according to Williams.

"This buck only shows himself one time a year, usually in the early afternoon when no one is hunting," Steve wrote. "He is usually seen from the windows of the house or car."

The huge whitetail had been within 15 to 20 yards of Lisa, but she suffered a bad case of buck fever and didn't fire a shot. Jack was posted 120 yards from Lisa and the buck went by him next. Jack took a shot at the buck with a slug from his 12 gauge shotgun, which turned the deer toward Mike. Mike was hunting with a .44 magnum handgun.

The buck stopped when 60 yards from Mike and he fired.

"Mike's .44 misfired twice," Steve explained, "and the lighting on his scope messed up, allowing the buck time to run back in the direction he came from and then into the cornfield."

Mike and Jack found hair and a little bit of blood where the buck had been when Mike took his shot, so he and Jack followed the whitetail into the corn. The snow that was on the ground made it easy to follow the deer. The spots of blood helped, too.

Lisa had remained on the edge of the cornfield while Jack and Mike followed the buck's tracks. She filled Steve and Hal in on what had happened when they arrived. After finding out what was going on, Steve and Hal took up positions at either end of the 20 acre cornfield, hoping to intercept the buck if it left the corn. Steve watched for deer with Lisa.

"Shortly after Hal got to the farthest end of the field, he started looking for tracks in the snow where the buck might have left the corn," Steve wrote. "That's when a small buck ran out of the field. A car passing on a nearby road scared the young buck and it ran toward Hal. When about 20 yards from Hal, that buck cut back into the corn. He didn't shoot because he was waiting to see if the big buck might appear.

"At the end of the field where Lisa and I were, two does ran out of the corn one way and a larger deer ran out another way. We found tiny drops of blood associated with the tracks of the larger deer, so we assumed that had been the big buck and he was gone for good. I then told Jack and Mike what we had seen.

"They, too, decided the buck was gone. They said it had been doing circles around them in the corn and there was only a small amount of blood here and there. They had been within six rows of the buck once, but it got up and ran off. Jack, Mike and Lisa then headed to the house for coffee.

"Hal decided we should hunt the corn to see if we could get the smaller buck he had seen run into the field. I had never hunted in a cornfield before. I had always hunted on the edge of fields. Hal told me to start at the place where he had seen the small buck enter the field and he would stay on the outside edge, just in case something ran out into the open again.

"After I was in the corn about 16 minutes, I looked through my binoculars and saw a large brown spot about 70 yards away. I moved over about four rows and walked 40 yards closer before taking another look. I couldn't tell if the brown spot was a deer, so I slid over one more row and moved 20 yards closer.

"I still couldn't tell until I put my head in the next row and saw antlers. I was less than 10 yards from the buck at that point. After I saw the antlers and knew I was looking at a buck, I pulled up my bolt action 16 gauge and shot the deer with a Winchester slug. I fell back and sat there for a minute as the deer ran off in a hurry.

"After a few minutes, I walked up to where the deer had been lying. I found hair, but no blood. I could tell where he had run because he knocked down the corn stalks all the way through. I followed the trail of downed stalks 30 yards and found blood. After going 20 yards further, I saw the buck and he was down!

"I finally saw the whole rack and it was big! I walked up and cautiously poked him with my gun to confirm he was dead. I grabbed the rack, not stopping to count the points, and tried to drag him out of the corn. I only made it two feet and gave up.

"I hurried out of the corn toward Hal, marking a trail, so I would be able to find the deer again. When I got to Hal, he asked me how many points the deer had. I told him I wasn't sure, that it was big and had at least six points on one side.

"Almost running, we returned to count 16 points on the big set of antlers. There was a hole through one of the buck's ears where Jack's slug had gone. There was also a strip of hair shaved off of his chest where Mike had hit him.

"I was smiling so much that day that I got a cramp in my jaw that wouldn't go away!"

Steve was wearing his grandfather's "lucky Realtree hunting suit" when he got his buck. The deer had a dressed weight of 170 pounds. The buck wasn't aged, but it was probably at least 4 1/2 years old.

The trophy whitetail was the fourth buck to Steve's credit. He got his first buck, a 3-pointer, with bow and arrow during 1998. The next year, he got an 8-pointer with a 13-inch spread during gun season while scrape hunting. He got another 3-point during the 2000 bow season.

This view of the left antler from the Williams Buck shows a pair of the nontypical points.

16 Is His Lucky Number

Steve Williams (right) and his stepfather Hal Heuer proudly display the head mount of Steve's trophy buck at the 2001 Michigan Deer Spectacular in Lansing after the rack won an award.

Photos courtesy Jake Jackovich

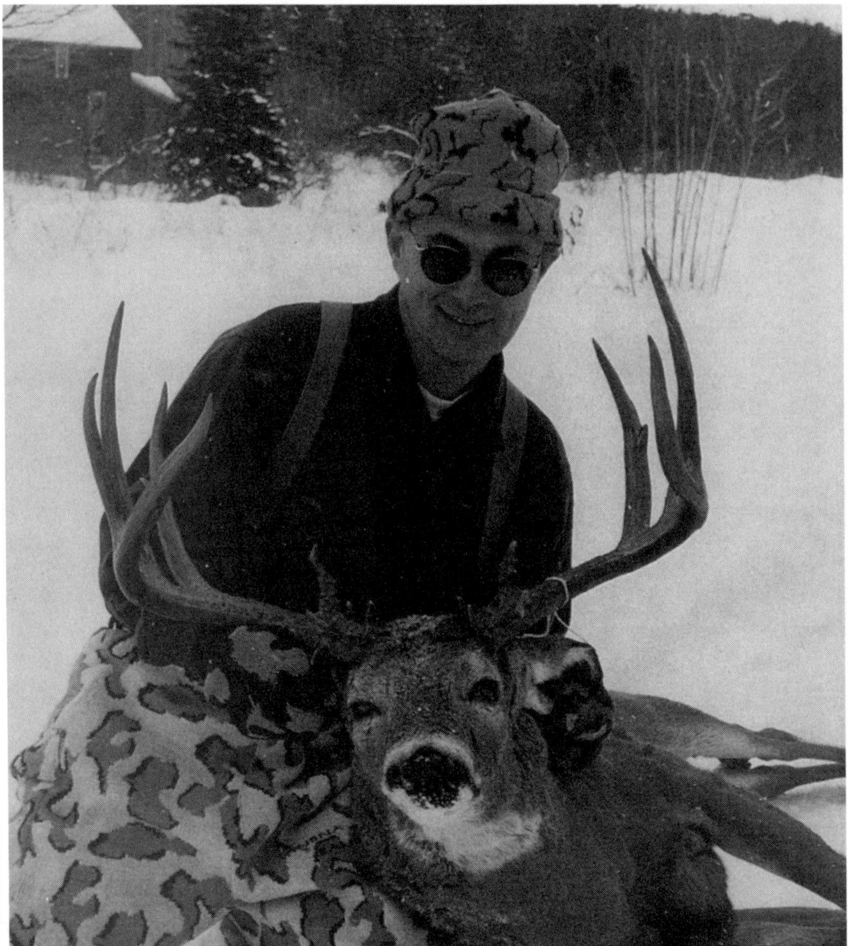

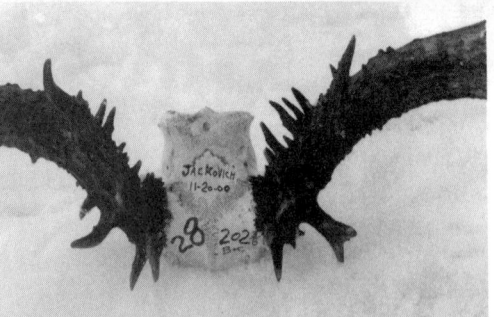

Jake Jackovich with Keweenaw County nontypical scoring 202 3/8 that he got in 2000. He missed the same buck two years earlier.

Most of the nontyical points on the Jackovich Buck are near the antler bases.

Chapter 8

Keweenaw County Nontypical

Friendly competition is common among deer hunting partners and it's no different between fathers and sons than other relatives and friends. So when Eric Jackovich bagged a trophy 10-pointer that scored 155 4/8 in the Upper Peninsula's Keweenaw County during 1997, it was natural for his father and hunting partner Bernard (Jake) from Calumet to vow he was going to get a bigger one. He almost accomplished the feat the following year, but he had to wait until the fall of 2000 to get a bigger buck than his son.

Jake not only beat his son's buck by a wide margin, he claimed a whitetail with the highest scoring nontypical rack known taken in the state during 2000 by a firearms hunter, according to state record keeper Commemorative Bucks of Michigan (CBM). Jackovich shot a Keweenaw County 26-pointer that had an official net score of 202 3/8. He thinks it's the same buck he almost got during 1998.

Also worthy of note is the Jackovich buck is the first booner recorded for the Upper Peninsula (U.P.) of Michigan since 1995. Nontypical racks must measure a minimum of 195 to qualify for a place in alltime national records maintained by the Boone and Crockett Club. Tim Spence from Brimley bagged a 24-pointer that scored 198 1/8 in Chippewa County during '95. The story about Spence's buck, along with two other nontypical booners from Chippewa County, are in Book 2 of Great Michigan Deer Tales.

Back-to-back severe winters in 1996 and 1997 are responsible for the absence of U.P. booners between 1996 and 1999. Winters started early and hung on late during 1995-'96 and 1996-'97. There were also record snowfalls both winters. Those winters were especially devastating because the U.P. deer population was at an alltime high during the fall of 1995 after a series of mild winters.

The DNR estimated that in excess of 200,000 deer died in the U.P. during the winter of 1995-'96. The toll was calculated to be a minimum of 110,000 the following winter. Many older age bucks died during those record setting winters and so did plenty of young ones. Adult bucks that survived were stressed and grew substandard antlers.

A series of mild winters between 1998 and 2000 allowed some bucks like the one Jake got, to attain ages where they are capable of producing their best antlers. The fact that supplemental winter deer feeding is a common practice on the Keweenaw Peninsula and remains legal today, helps many bucks there not only survive winter, but generate excellent antler development, even during severe winters. Supplemental winter deer feeding was banned by the DNR in all U.P. counties starting in 2004, with the exception of those in the Lake Superior Watershed.

U.P. bucks seldom produce racks large enough to make B&C listing until they are at least 5 1/2 years old. Mild conditions and supplemental feeding not only allow more bucks to survive winter, reduced nutritional stress permits those that survive to realize their maximum antler growth potential.

The last typicals from the U.P. that met the B&C minimum of 170 were taken during 1994. Daniel Coponen got an 11-point that measured 174 5/8 in Houghton County that year and Lanny Higley also nailed a 16-pointer that scored 172 7/8 in Schoolcraft County.

Jake's big nontypical ranked third among gun kills in Keweenaw County in that category, at the time this was written. Bernie Murn collected the county's highest scoring nontypical during 1980, a 23-pointer that netted 218 1/8. The story behind Murn's B&C buck can be found in Book 1 of <u>Great Michigan Deer Tales</u>. Nathan Ruonavaara shot an 18-point during 1946 that currently ranks second among nontypicals in the county with a score of 209 1/8.

"Eric was my inspiration," Jackovich said about his son. "We hunted a lot together. After he got that 10-pointer that scored 155, I told him I was going to get a bigger one. That was a standing joke around here.

"But I got a shot at a buck on opening day of the 1998 season that I think would have beat Eric's deer. A doe came across a skid trail that I was watching where there was a scrape line. I caught movement behind her and here comes this big bodied deer.

"Instead of crossing the skid trail, he angled to my right in thick brush. He had a wide, high rack. He was looking right at me and I had the rifle up. I tried to put a bullet through the brush with my Ruger .243, but it didn't make it. I found the branch that deflected the bullet after tracking him in the snow and not finding any sign of a hit."

Jake was hunting in the same spot during the fall of 2000 when he got the booner. That's why he suspects the buck he missed might be the same one he eventually got.

"I've hunted deer all of my life," Jackovich said. "I love to hunt deer. I love to eat venison. I've been deer hunting since 1965, with the exception of a couple of years I was in the Marine Corps.

"I'm a combat veteran from Viet Nam. I was seriously injured over there. I lost my right leg below the knee and lost the use of my left hand, but I still get around good in the woods and I can shoot a gun okay, too."

Jake wears an artificial limb to replace the missing portion of his right leg. It's made of carbon fibers and only weighs about 2 pounds. He said the carbon fitting is much better than the wooden replacement he used to wear, which weighed as much as 8 pounds.

A silicone stump sock Jackovich now wears is also better than the wool models he used to use because they reduce abrasion. That's something that is extremely important for some one who is as active as Jake is. Besides being an active whitetail hunter, he does a lot of cross country skiing. He completed a 26-mile cross country ski race with his daughter during the winter after he got his big buck.

If you assumed that Jake does most of his deer hunting from a stand due to his artificial leg, you would be wrong.

"I prefer stillhunting," he said. "I don't bait. I don't use a blind.

I just like to hunt sign and try to go one-on-one with them. I like to hunt scrapes.

"The rifle I was hunting with when I got the nontypical is an old Ruger .44 magnum carbine that was handed down in the family. It was my late father-in-law's gun. He was just an old stillhunter. He just went out and walked around in the woods and just hunted the deer down. I guess I'm just keeping up the tradition."

Prior to 2000, the best bucks to Jake's credit were a pair of 8-points that would score around 105. Of course, he was more interested in collecting venison during most of his deer hunting career instead of a set of trophy antlers. As mentioned earlier, that changed during 1997.

Although most of Jake's deer hunting has been with a rifle, he's also done some bow hunting. He bagged a pair of whitetails with a Browning compound bow while hunting from a tree stand. His first bow kill was a doe. His second was a forkhorn.

"That was kind of a milestone for me," Jackovich said, "hunting from a tree stand and getting a couple of deer with bow and arrow. The bones in my left hand were shattered, so it's hard for me to use that hand in cold weather."

Jake's resolve about bagging a trophy buck was stronger than ever during 2000 after finding the tracks of a big buck in his hunting area.

"I knew he was around," he said. "I found a scrape line and a big track, so I let some other bucks pass. I saw six other bucks on the same trail the big buck was using. Two of them had 4-points, two had 6s and a couple were small 8s. If I had shot one of them, I think there's a good chance I might not have gotten the big one."

It was on the afternoon of November 20th that Jake scored on the booner.

"I picked up his track at 3:00 p.m.," Jackovich said. "We had a good snow storm going on. Snow was coming down heavy. I knew he was going to make a rounder through the swamp and come back and check his scrapes. I had a hunch he would come through and it paid off.

"I sat against an old oak blowdown and I blended in well. The wind was in my favor. He came through at 4:30 at a fast trot. All of a sudden,

I saw a flash of brown movement. I managed to bring my gun up and took the safety off. When he came into the first opening, I hit him right behind the shoulder and that put him down. It happened that fast.

"I didn't have time to see how big he was. He came out of the thick stuff at 35 yards. This is the one I was waiting for.

"I told my wife I would like to get something to mount this year. I guess it happened.

"When I shot the buck, I didn't gut it or anything. I knew I would need help to get it out of the woods. When I called my son and told him I finally got a buck bigger than his, he thought I was pulling his leg. That changed when he saw the buck."

The whitetail had a dressed weight of 189 pounds and was aged at 5 1/2. The buck had a hunk out of his left ear and a couple of scars on his neck from fighting, so Jake is anxious to see the deer it had been fighting with. There may be another big one around.

In fact, Jackovich knows there are other trophy bucks in Keweenaw County. He saw one of them during the December muzzleloader season. He saw a big 10-pointer that was definitely in the 150 class. Jake trailed that deer for two hours in deep snow, but never managed to get a shot at it before he got tired.

He also heard about another whitetail with antlers similar to the one he shot. A logger had seen it and described the rack. Jake was hoping his son would get that whitetail, but they never saw it.

The 26-pointer that Jackovich shot in 2000 has a typical 10-point frame with lots of short sticker points at the base of the antlers. There are a total of 15 points on the left antler and 11 on the right. Ten of the tines on the left antler are nontypicals and there are 6 nontypicals on the right side.

Most of the sticker points are between one and two inches long. The total length of all nontypical points is 21 1/8 inches. Four of the main tines are over 12 inches long, the beams exceed 27 inches in length and the inside spread is 22 4/8. The rack only had 2 4/8 inches of deductions.

Pat Abram with the Boone and Crockett nontypical he bagged in Mackinac County on November 16, 2000 that was 8 1/2-years-old.

Chapter 9

8-Year-Old Booner From The U.P.

A pair of Boone and Crockett qualifying bucks were bagged in the U.P. during the fall of 2000. Both were nontypicals. One was taken in the western portion of the region and the other was taken in the east. Jake Jackovich from Calumet got the one from the west and his hunt is covered in the previous chapter. Pat Abram from Curtis scored on the one to the east and this chapter is about his success on the buck he got.

Abram met with success in Mackinac County on November 16, 2000. The buck he got has 16 points and tremendous mass, generating an official net score of 196 2/8. The whitetail's age was as impressive as its antlers. The deer was 8 1/2 years old.

Very few bucks in Michigan live to that age. Those that are born in the U.P. have a better chance of reaching old age than bucks that spend their lives in the rest of the state. A number of bucks that have been older than 8 1/2 have been recorded from the U.P. One of the chapters in Book 1 of Great Michigan Deer Tales is about some of the oldest deer on record for the state. A chapter in Book 3 of the series is about an Iron County buck that also lived to be 8 1/2 before he was bagged by a hunter.

However, the Iron County buck's antlers didn't grow large

enough to qualify for state records, much less Boone and Crockett. That whitetail was a trophy nonetheless and serves as an example to illustrate that not all bucks are capable of growing large racks, no matter how old they get.

The Abram Buck is the second highest scoring nontypical on record for Mackinac County. The county's number one nontypical is a 27-pointer shot in 1951 by Donald Van Doornik. Those antlers net 205 2/8.

One factor that played an important role in Pat Abram's success on his Boone and Crockett buck during the fall of 2000 is he passed up a young buck minutes before the booner appeared. Pat let a yearling forkhorn go five minutes before the once-in-a-lifetime whitetail came walking along. If he had shot the young whitetail, there's a good chance he would not have had the opportunity at the much bigger deer.

Also worthy of note about the hunt on which Abram got his impressive 16-pointer on November 16, is he only hunted the last hour of daylight. It was 4:45 p.m. by the time he climbed into his tree stand overlooking the intersection of several runways surrounded by thick popple (aspen) saplings. He said the saplings were so thick he could only see 50 feet into them. The elevated stand gave him a better view than if he were on the ground.

Pat said he shot a 7-pointer from the stand during 1999, so he knew the spot was a good one. He said he didn't see any deer on opening day, probably because one that was approaching his stand winded him. It stood where it was after smelling the hunter and snorted for 15 minutes, alerting any whitetail within hearing about potential danger.

Abram said the primary reason he went deer hunting on the evening of November 16th was to provide moral support for his son. And that support worked in the boy's favor. Soon after Pat climbed into his stand, he heard his son shoot. He later found out the boy got a 3-pointer.

It was about 5:30 when Abram saw the buck with small antlers. As a veteran hunter with plenty of whitetails to his credit, he wasn't interested in shooting the young buck. The fact that he thought his son might already have a deer down may have played a role in his decision, too, but the important point is he waited.

At 5:35, he saw another deer. It was walking straight toward him on a skid trail.

"I thought it was a doe at first," Pat said. "I couldn't see antlers. Then I put my rifle to my shoulder, so I could look at it through the scope. I saw antlers right way through the scope. I knew it was a darn good rack, too, but I wasn't sure just how big it was."

The buck was 75 yards away when Abram took careful aim with his .308 and fired, dropping the whitetail instantly. Pat was in for the surprise of his life when he walked up to the dead deer and saw exactly how big the antlers were.

"I've never seen a deer with horns like that around here, ever," he said.

However, a school bus driver saw the buck in 2000, according to Abram, two weeks before firearms season opened. The bus driver watched the buck follow a doe across a field. He told Pat the deer's antlers were high and heavy. The guy thought the beams were as wide as his hand. The bus driver accurately described the whitetail that Pat later got.

At least one other hunter, an archer, got a shot at the trophy buck before Pat did. When Abram butchered the whitetail, he found a softball-size mass of green gristle encasing a broadhead that had penetrated the buck's left shoulder blade. Fortunately for Pat, the bowhunter's aim hadn't been better. The wound was totally healed, so the arrow had connected at least a year earlier and probably even before that.

"I've always been suspicious that the buck I got was one that a young man up the road hit with an arrow four years earlier," Abram said. "He shot a decent buck and they didn't bring anything with them to finish it off when they trailed it. The buck was still alive when they saw it and then it took off. No remains of that deer were ever found.

"That arrow wound was nearly fatal. It was still possible to see that all of the tissue on the ribs was lacerated from him running with that broadhead. Where that guy shot the buck with bow and arrow was only 100 yards from where the school bus driver saw the one I got before gun season."

Pat said the antlers from his B&C buck actually have 21 projections that could be called points, but five of them are less than an inch long. Points have to be at least an inch long to be considered for official scoring purposes. He added that another point was broken off near the end of the right beam.

The rack has 10 official points on one beam and six on the other. When first measured after the 60-day drying period, the antlers scored 194 7/8, 1/8-of-an-inch less than the B&C minimum. However, when it was later panel measured, the final score was 196 2/8, more than an inch over the magic number of 195.

One thing that really stands out about the Abram Buck is the exceptional mass of the antlers. The circumference of the base of the right antler is 5 inches and the left antler measures 5 2/8 inches, but the beams are much thicker between the second and third typical points. The third circumference on the right antler is 5 6/8 inches versus 6 6/8 inches on the left antler.

The total of circumference measurements on most racks is less than 40 inches. That total for the Abram Buck is 42 5/8.

Beam lengths aren't anything out of the ordinary, with the right one taping 25 1/8 inches and the left 24 2/8. Inside spread is 19 1/8 inches. The third typical tine on the right side is the longest at 13 inches and the G4 is 11 inches in length. Both the G3 and 4 on the left side are over 11 inches long.

There are five nontypical points on the right antler and three on the left. One of the nontypical tines on the left antler is 10 2/8 inches long. Total lengths of the nontypical points is 28 6/8 inches.

The buck had a big body besides an exceptional rack. The whitetail had a dressed weight of 197 pounds.

Pat's best buck prior to the fall of 2000 was a big-bodied 8-pointer that he got with bow and arrow in Mackinac County during 1988. Its body size was more impressive than its antlers. The deer had a dressed weight of 230 pounds and the antlers measured 110 4/8. Abram's son shot the 3-point he got in 2000 from the same stand where Pat scored on that 8.

The stand consists of a platform between a pair of balsam trees that's 22 feet from the ground. Extra boughs from the balsams are used in front of the platform to camouflage hunters.

Abram said he missed what would have been his best buck prior to the fall of 2000 while bowhunting during late December of 1998 over bait. He got a shot at a trophy animal that had a wide rack with at least 14 points. The tines were six to eight inches long. Pat estimated the width of that buck's rack at 24 inches.

"I had to watch that buck for over an hour before he got to the bait," Abram remembered. "It was a real quiet evening. I was hunting with a recurve bow and wooden arrows. The buck was only 13 1/2 yards away when I released an arrow."

Pat shoots instinctively with his 62 pound pull Jim Brackenbury recurve, so instinct took over when he finally had the opportunity for a shot. He was so used to shooting at 20 yards that he released the arrow as though the deer was 20 yards away and his homemade arrow sailed an inch over the buck's back.

"He took a couple of jumps to get behind a maple tree after I missed him," Pat continued. "He stood there for a while and then walked off. Some times during the late season, we get migratory deer moving through the area. That buck was definitely a stranger.

"If that buck had been 20 yards away, I would have drilled him through the lungs. I'm used to practicing at 20 yards."

It can be difficult to impossible to determine when or if you might have a chance at a booner. The only way to up the odds in your favor is to hunt every chance you get, even if it's only for an hour, and be persistent. It also helps to pass up small bucks and to practice shooting at different distances, if you are a bowhunter.

Brian Kessman with Michigan's best typical from 2002, an 11-pointer that nets 182 1/8.

Chapter 10

2002's Best Typical

Southern Michigan's Jackson County has produced some of our state's highest scoring whitetails over the years and the county lived up to its reputation again during the fall of 2002 by producing the highest scoring typical-antlered buck known taken in the state that year, according to state record keeper Commemorative Bucks of Michigan (CBM). Brian Kessman from Horton bagged that deer with a shotgun on opening day of firearms season. The 11-pointer has a gross score of 189 2/8 and nets 182 1/8.

The current state record typical came from the same county in 1996 and the following year another typical that occupies the number three spot in CBM records was collected within that county's borders. Troy Stephens of Jackson got the number one typical in '96 with a borrowed shotgun in an area he had never hunted before. The massive 16-pointer had an amazing gross score of 214 3/8 and netted 198. The particulars about the hunt on which that buck was taken can be found in Book 2 of <u>Great Michigan Deer Tales</u>.

Rick Hanson from Napoleon connected on the Jackson County 10-pointer during 1997 that now ranks third among typicals in state records. His story is in Book 3 of <u>Great Michigan Deer Tales</u>. The antlers from Michigan's Hanson Buck had a gross score of 193 4/8 and netted 188 1/8. Hanson shot his buck from an area where he had scored on a number of smaller bucks over the years.

Among typical bucks bagged in Jackson County, Kessman's will fall in the number three spot in state records behind the whitetails taken by Stephens and Hanson. On a statewide basis, the Kessman buck ranked eighth among typical gun kills at the time it was taken. About a dozen bucks from Jackson County that are large enough to qualify for national records maintained by the Boone and Crockett Club (scoring at least 170 for typicals and 195 for nontypicals) are listed in CBM records and more world class bucks are sure to come from the county in the future.

Among the booners currently recorded for Jackson County, 10 are typicals and two are nontypicals. Four of the typicals and one of the nontypicals were taken by bowhunters. Charles Sullivan from Grass Lake has the highest scoring typical bow kill from the county listed in CBM records. It's a 10-point that he arrowed during November of 2000 that nets 180 1/8.

Brian Kessman makes no secret about the fact there was a lot of luck involved in the taking of his big buck in 2002. He hadn't seen the deer before the day he got it and his objective when he went afield during the afternoon of November 15 was not to shoot a deer at all. He planned on scouting for the next day's hunt. However, when he was presented with the opportunity to shoot the buck of a lifetime, he was more than willing to take advantage of being in the right place at the right time.

Michigan's biggest typical for 2002 was Brian's first Michigan buck, but it wasn't his first whitetail. That year was the 28-year-old's sixth year of deer hunting, but his first to try for whitetails in Michigan. Brian's first five years of whitetail hunting were spent in Virginia, where he was very successful.

He tagged a dozen bucks during those years, most of which were taken while hunting with a rifle. His best buck prior to coming to Michigan was a 120 class 8-point.

Kessman moved to Michigan during May of 2002 with his wife and young son. He did some bowhunting, taking a doe on opening day of archery season (October 1).

Although he didn't connect on any bucks while bowhunting, he saw some with nice racks. The buck sightings during bow season had Brian primed for firearms season.

On opening morning of gun season, Brian hunted with an uncle.

Kessman saw three bucks and three does. He said he saw the first buck before it was light enough to see well. He could make out antlers on the deer's head, but couldn't tell how big they were. It wasn't yet shooting time anyway, so he let it go.

Brian's uncle shot a nice 8-point at 8:30 a.m. that dressed out at 183 pounds. Kessman thinks that may have been the antlered whitetail that went by him before legal shooting time.

It was light enough to see well when Brian saw a second buck. It had a small odd-shaped rack and Kessman probably would not have taken that deer either. However, he didn't have a chance to turn it down. The buck saw him move and it spooked.

Brian saw a 6-point about 8:45 that he could have shot, but he decided to pass it up. By then he knew his uncle had scored and the bigger deer he saw while bowhunting gave him the incentive to wait. That was the first antlered buck that was legal to shoot that he passed up.

A friend of Brian's was supposed to arrive to hunt with him on the evening of the 15th. After the morning hunt, he considered waiting around the house for his friend to arrive. However, his wife Tracy talked him into going back out hunting late in the day, so he decided to make a scouting trip out of it.

"I set up in a tree overlooking two fields," Kessman said. "I wanted to see where deer were moving. There are only two or three bedding areas in that location. I figured I could get a good idea where my friend should hunt based on what I saw.

"I was in the tree about an hour," Brian continued, "when I looked over my right shoulder and saw a doe in the woods. I guess I moved too fast. She spooked and ran off. There was a buck behind her. I saw his antlers as he was running away. I knew I just blew a chance at a great big buck.

"Thirty minutes later I looked over my left shoulder and saw the doe again. After I spotted the doe, I saw the buck slip into some cover where I couldn't see him. When the doe went behind a tree I turned and got in position for a shot at the buck when he reappeared.

"Then it was just a matter of waiting the buck out. I could see all the way around the thick patch of brush the buck went in, so there was no way he was going to leave it without me seeing him.

My bare hands were getting cold by the time I saw him again. The temperature was in the 20s and there was a strong wind.

"It was 20 minutes after the buck disappeared from view when he finally crossed a lane about 75 yards away. When I shot, he kicked out with his hind legs and took off."

Brian was hunting with an Ithaca 12 gauge shotgun that has open sights. He was using a rifled Deer Slayer barrel. The gun was loaded with 2 3/4-inch Barnes Expander sabot slugs.

"The buck came within 60 yards of me as he was running," Kessman said, "and I shot a second time with buckshot, but I think I missed with that shot. I found a lot of blood when I climbed down from the tree, so I knew I made a good hit on the buck. I followed the blood trail about 100 yards and didn't find the deer. It was getting late, so I decided to call for help.

"I called my wife and mother and then my stepbrother. They wanted to come out and help me find the deer, so I waited for them to arrive. It was dark by the time they got there, but they brought flashlights to use to find the deer."

They didn't have to follow the buck much farther before finding it after Brian's family arrived. The buck ran an estimated 125 yards after it was shot.

"I fell to my knees when I knew he was dead," Kessman commented. "I simply knelt there and admired the big buck. I didn't touch it for 10 to 15 minutes.

"I had five of my closest family members with me when I first laid eyes on the dead buck and his huge antlers. It was a delight to have them there with me!

"That's the biggest deer I've ever seen," Brian added. "I've never been around a Boone and Crockett buck before. I thought the antlers might score in the 160s or 170. I didn't have a clue how big they really were."

The exceptional whitetail was not one of the bucks that Brian had seen while bowhunting. After he got the deer, he talked to other people who said they had seen it. He originally called the buck a 12-point, but one of the those points didn't end up being long enough to be an official point. Tines have to be at least an inch long to be considered in official measurements. The twelfth point was 6/8-of-an-inch long.

The rack has a 10-point frame with exceptional tine length. The brow tines are at least 8 inches long, both G2s are more than 13 inches long and the G3s are over 10 inches in length. The eleventh point is a nontypical tine on the base of the right antler that is 3 6/8 inches in length. The other projection that is less than an inch long is near the nontypical tine.

Besides long tines, the rack had exceptional beam length. The right beam is 29 1/8 inches long and the left is 27 4/8. Inside spread between the antlers is 19 5/8 inches.

The big buck had a dressed weight of 210 pounds. It was probably at least 4 1/2 years old. Since Brian said he never expected to get a whitetail that big, his success was definitely a surprise. He did pretty good for what was supposed to simply be a scouting mission.

Brian Kessman with his Jackson County booner.

Jason Newman at 22 years old with his 20-point nontypical bow kill from Allegan County. The antlers from his buck net 195 4/8.

Chapter 11

The Newman Buck

Jason Newman from Otsego was the second Michigan bowhunter in as many years to bag a buck with a nontypical rack large enough to qualify for national records maintained by the Boone and Crockett Club. The impressive 20-pointer he arrowed on November 6, 1994 in Allegan County had a point for almost every year of the young hunter's life. Jason was 22 when he got the booner that had a gross score of 201 and net score of 195 4/8, a half-inch more than the minimum for entry in Boone and Crockett Records.

The buck also easily qualifies for listing in national bowhunting records compiled by the Pope and Young Club. The minimum for nontypical whitetail antlers to make it into P&Y records is 150. A score of 125 is all that is needed to be put into state records maintained by Commemorative Bucks of Michigan (CBM).

Herb Miller from Brooklyn was the first Michigan archer to claim a nontypical booner in the state, according to CBM Records, and he succeeded in doing so on November 8, 1993. The 22-pointer he tagged in Jackson County measured 196 7/8. The story about how Miller got his buck is in Book 2 of <u>Great Michigan Deer Tales</u>. It was an amazing coincidence that so many years went by without a buck of that caliber being taken by a bowhunter and then to have it happen two years in a row.

Although it was rare for bowhunters to bag B&C bucks in the early to mid-1990s, especially those with nontypical antlers, times have changed. Between 1994 and 2005, when this was written, no less than nine more B&C nontypicals had been tagged by bowhunters in Michigan, resulting in the state record in that category changing hands a number of times. Another chapter in this book is devoted to the hunt and hunter behind one of the more recent state record nontypical bow kills. Stories behind other bucks in that class are in Books 2 and 3.

One of the reasons archers are accounting for more world class bucks now than they used to is bowhunting is more popular. Even more important though, is that bowhunters are more knowledgeable about what it takes to connect on trophy bucks such as being persistent, hunting during the rut and passing up small bucks.

Another factor that I think is involved is that there are more bucks with big racks available in the state than there used to be, especially those with nontypical racks, and bowhunters are starting to get some of them. And archers are certainly not the only hunters cashing in on what appears to be an increase in nontypical booners in the state. CBM measurers put tapes to eight B&C qualifiers that were shot during the 1994 gun season and three of those were nontypicals. Still one more nontypical that was the largest of the lot was found dead after deer season ended. Firearms hunters have traditionally taken the bulk of the biggest bucks bagged in the state every year.

For a while, it appeared as though Newman's buck was going to break the record set the year before for nontypical bow kills by Miller. The green score of the rack from Jason's buck soon after he got it was 198 3/8. Before an official score can be obtained for antlers, they must air dry for 60 days. There was speculation that the final score for the Newman head would be better than 196 7/8, but that obviously didn't happen.

The fact that the antlers from his buck were not a new state record didn't matter to Jason. He was not disappointed at all. Who would be after taking a book buck like that with bow and arrow?

"I just wanted one for the wall," Newman said. "I'm more than satisfied. I would have shot a spike, if I would have seen one. I'm not picky."

With only three years of bowhunting for deer under his belt at

The Newman Buck

the time, Jason had no reason to be picky, although he's certainly done better than most archers with that amount of experience. He arrowed a 5-pointer during his first year of bowhunting on October 2, 1992. He got his second bow-bagged whitetail on the same date during 1994, a doe.

Newman said he had a lot more experience deer hunting with a shotgun than bow and arrow by 1994. He started pursuing whitetails with a gun when he was 14 and, as mentioned earlier, he was 22 when he scored on the big buck. Jason said he had taken about a dozen deer during eight years of gun hunting.

Interestingly, he also got his best buck with a gun during the fall of 1994, so it was his best year ever as a whitetail hunter. The 8-pointer he dropped with buckshot from a borrowed shotgun during a drive on November 25, 1994 is certainly not in the same league with his best bow kill though. The buck that grew the 8-point rack was a young one.

Jason says he likes bowhunting for deer much better than gun hunting because he sees far more deer. The tree stand he shot his trophy buck from with bow and arrow is on property his family owns and he said he put it up during the spring of 1994. He added that he likes to put new tree stands up during the spring versus summer or fall because he can avoid interference from mosquitoes and it reduces the chances of disturbing local deer close to the time he plans on hunting.

He put the stand where he did based on deer sightings the previous fall while bowhunting. A lot of the whitetails he saw were out of bow range, so he figured an adjustment in positions was in order. There are a lot of oak trees on the property and the acorns the trees produce usually attract plenty of whitetails. If deer movements were the same during 1994 as they were the year before, Jason figured he would get a decent bow shot, but he never dreamed of releasing an arrow at such a tremendous buck.

On the day he got the booner, Newman headed toward his stand about 1:00 p.m. He wore waders that day so he could walk down a creek to the stand. The primary reason he walked in the creek is to see if he could sneak up on any bucks that might be bedded along its banks, but he didn't see any.

His water approach may have served another more important function that he didn't consider. He would have kept contamination of the area around his stand from his scent to a minimum. The less human scent in the area, the less cautious or suspicious whitetails will be, especially older animals that have survived several hunting seasons. It's difficult to determine if Jason's use of the creek that day played a role in his exceptional success, but it might have.

Most of Newman's vigil that afternoon and evening was basically uneventful. So much so that he dozed off. He woke up about 5:15 p.m. to see a buck about 75 yards away. Noise the deer might have made could have been what aroused Jason.

He only got a glimpse of antler. Based on what he saw, he thought it was a small buck, but he didn't care. He was interested in trying for it, if he could get a shot.

Jason had been sitting on a folding chair. When he saw the whitetail, he stood up, folding the chair and leaned it against the tree to get it out of the way. He winced when it fell over, fearing the noise would scare the deer, but the whitetail didn't seem to react. Fortunately, the deer was far enough away that the blunder didn't make any difference.

Newman had at least three different deer calls with him and he tried them all in an effort to lure the buck within bow range. He said he blew into his Micro Grunt and Heat N' Bleat Calls first and got no reaction. The buck finally came toward him after he blew into his Big River Game Call.

It may have actually been the combination of calls that brought the bruiser in to investigate. Based on the variety of calls Jason used, the whitetail may have thought a couple of bucks were vying for a doe in heat. As a dominant buck, the trophy animal probably couldn't resist the temptation to find out what was going on.

The buck's curiosity cost him his life. When the whitetail trotted into an opening 35 yards away, Jason released an arrow from his 85 pound pull Martin bow, scoring a good hit, although he didn't know it at the time. The shaft was tipped with a 125 grain Muzzy broadhead.

Jason knew he had just shot a trophy buck, but he didn't know how much of a trophy. At the time he took the shot, he thought the antlers had 10 or 12 points. He last saw the buck on the edge of a field.

Unsure of how badly the buck was hurt, Jason went to get his father and they returned to search for the whitetail. The bowhunter's father spotted the world class buck not far from where Jason last saw it and called his son over. Both of them had a hard time believing the dimensions of the impressive antlers when they reached the dead deer.

The rack has a typical 10-point frame, with 10 nontypical tines. Six of the nontypicals are on the right antler and four are on the left. Total length of the nontypical points is 31 7/8 inches.

The right beam is 25 6/8 inches long and the left is 24 inches. The beam tips curve around toward each other, coming fairly close together. There's only 4 1/8 inches between the tips of the antlers. The inside spread between the antlers isn't exceptional either, only measured 15 3/8 inches.

The second and third typical tines on the left antler are over 10 inches long. The same tines on the right beam are over nine inches in length. All of the circumference measurements are between four and five inches.

There was some celebrating in the Newman household that evening. The buck was estimated to be between 5 1/2 and 7 1/2 years old and had a dressed weight of 197 pounds. It's a fine whitetail that any bowhunter would be proud of.

The rack from Newman's buck ranked second among nontypical bow kills in Michigan at the time it was scored. By 2005, it ranked 12th among nontypical bow kills in CBM records. The antlers are currently in third place among nontypicals for Allegan County. Jon West bagged the county's number one nontypical, a 30-pointer, during the 1984 gun season that scores 231 1/8, according to CBM records. Bruce Maurer got a 21-pointer scoring 210 4/8 from the county with a shotgun during 1997.

The story behind the Maurer Buck is in Book 3 of <u>Great Michigan Deer Tales</u>.

Photo courtesy Mario VanderMeulen

Mario VanderMeulen with his Saginaw County booner scoring 170 1/8. Note the short drop tine on the left antler.

Chapter 12

Saginaw County Booner

Like many Michigan whitetail hunters, Mario VanderMeulen from Birch Run dreamed of bagging a trophy buck some day. However, when he wasn't dreaming, he accepted what he thought was the harsh reality that the odds of actually accomplishing the feat were slim to none. As it turns out, his dream wasn't so unrealistic after all.

He got his dream buck on November 26, 1999 near his home in Saginaw County and the antlers on that deer just might be bigger than those he had been dreaming about. The 12-pointer scores 170 1/8, according to Commemorative Bucks of Michigan (CBM). That score easily surpasses the minimum of 125 for entry of typical racks in state records and is also high enough to qualify for national records maintained by the Boone and Crockett Club. The B&C minimum is 170.

Mario's buck is the second highest scoring typical entered in state records from the 1999 season, according to CBM, and ranked fourth among typicals for Saginaw County at the time this was written. Scott Hutchins, also from Birch Run, bagged another 12-pointer from the county during 1990 that measured 170 4/8. Orrin Nothelfer from Freeland got an 11-pointer during 2000 that nets 174. The county's number one typical is another 11-point scoring 179 3/8 that Carl Stockford shot during the 1969 firearms season.

The booner that Orrin Nothelfer got in Saginaw County the

year after Mario got his was also taken toward the end of gun season. Nothelfer connected on November 29th. Orrin said he and his brother Norris decided to go out on the next to the last day of the season that year in spite of the fact they hadn't seen many deer earlier and it obviously paid off handsomely.

The trophy buck that neither Nothelfer had seen before, was following a doe when Orrin dropped it with a pair of slugs from his 10 gauge shotgun. Although Orrin said he wasn't enthused about hunting that day, this is a perfect example of how persistence can pay off when after whitetails. Deer often appear when least expected. A change in weather or hunting pressure, as well as any number of other factors, which can't always be anticipated, can make all of the difference.

Scott Hutchins got his B&C buck from the county on the second day of the 1990 gun season. He was hunting with Dusty Sparks from Clio that day. Sparks pushed the buck out of a cornfield and into Hutchins' sights at a distance of 60 yards.

Mario had 10 years of deer hunting experience in 1999, starting with a shotgun when he was 14 years old. He was 24 when he got his dream buck. At the time, he had been a three season hunter for five or six years. That's how long he had been bowhunting for whitetails. He also hunts deer with a muzzleloader during the December season.

Although VanderMeulen hadn't been successful in taking a trophy buck prior to the fall of 1999, he had taken his share of smaller bucks. He said he had shot at least 20 deer since he started hunting and all but one of them were bucks. He tagged the one doe during muzzleloader season.

"Most of the bucks I've shot have been 4s or 6s, with a few spikes and 3s," Mario said. "My first buck was an 8-pointer. It was my best buck until 1999."

All of the deer VanderMeulen had shot, except for the big one, have come from 150 acres of land his parents own near Tawas City. Whitetail numbers are much higher there than near his home. That's where he got the 8-point when he was 15 years old.

Mario and his father were staying in a motor home on the property at the time. The boy was hunting with a 20 gauge pump shotgun.

"I had a heater in the blind," VanderMeulen remembered. "At one point, I accidentally kicked the heater when I shifted positions and it went out. I thought for sure the noise would spook any deer around.

"So I was packing up and getting ready to leave, but I looked around before leaving and a buck came running up. I was surprised to see that deer, but I took advantage of the opportunity to get my first buck. It was a thrill!

"I remember my Dad was driving an El Camino at the time. He tore the exhaust off of it while driving on the property to pick up my deer."

The VanderMeulens built a cabin on the property to hunt from the following year and have enjoyed continued success there.

"Everyone in my family has shot several deer up there, so that was where we always went to hunt because we were almost guaranteed a deer," Mario commented.

Although there were fewer deer near home, VanderMeulen started spending more time hunting there prior to 1999. The advantage of hunting close to home is he could spend some time afield even when he only had an hour or two. And he knew there were some big bucks in the area.

His father had gotten a big 9-pointer in the vicinity during 1986. The antlers from that buck were never measured, but, based on their size compared to the one Mario got in 1999, he guessed the rack would score in the 150s.

While scouting for potential stand sites during the 1999 bow season, Mario found a hot spot. He found an excellent deer trail that was well traveled and it had plenty of buck sign. He found 10 rubs and scrapes in a 30 yard radius.

With the help of his wife, he positioned a ladder stand in that location. They put the stand about 15 yards from the deer trail, so any whitetails using it would be within easy bow range. The 12-foot-high stand also gave Mario a view of the area along the trail where buck sign was abundant.

"I had been out a few times in that stand during bow and firearm season, but I hadn't seen any bucks," Mario said. "I had only seen a few does. I was hunting from the ladder stand again on Friday evening, November 26. I heard some noises on and off all evening that proved to only be squirrels and a raccoon. Then, about 5:10 p.m., I heard noise that I knew wasn't made by a small animal.

"All of a sudden, three deer appeared on the trail about 35 yards in front of me," Mario continued. "My heart started to race until I could identify all three deer as does. But they were more curious about what was coming behind them than keeping an eye on me or the trail ahead and that kept my heart rate up.

"Anticipating another deer, I got my shotgun ready, hoping something would appear soon since it was getting dark. It wasn't long before a buck stepped out of the thick woods. Without hesitating, I raised the gun and took the shot before I had a heart attack from all the anticipation!"

Although confident of a good hit on the buck, Mario waited a few minutes in his stand before climbing down to look for the deer. The wait helped him calm down after the excitement. The hunter's confidence in a good hit was reinforced when he reached the spot where the buck had been standing when he shot. He encountered good blood there and started following it.

"I walked for about 50 yards through the woods while following the blood, when the trail made a sharp turn," VanderMeulen explained. "After I turned the corner, I got the surprise of a liftetime, seeing that monster buck just laying there. I almost tripped on him. He was laying right in the trail. I had no idea he was that big when I shot him."

The 2 3/4-inch Winchester slug that Mario fired from his iron-sighted 12 gauge Remington semi-automatic had done a good job. Once he saw the size of the big buck, VanderMeulen knew he would need help to gut it and get it home. His father was hunting up north, so he called his Uncle Jerry and Aunt Terry for help and they kindly obliged.

The big whitetail had a dressed weight of 185 pounds and its age was estimated at 5 1/2. When Mario's uncle saw the buck, he thought it might have been the same one he saw the previous Tuesday when hunting two miles away. When he saw the buck, it was at least 300 yards from him, but Jerry still didn't have any trouble seeing its huge

Saginaw County Booner

antlers.

The 12-point rack on Mario's buck has 10 typical tines and two nontypical or sticker points. One of the stickers is a short drop tine that comes off the bottom of the left beam. The second nontypical point that's over an inch long is on the base of the right antler below the brow tine.

Both beams are over 28 inches long, which adds a lot to the score. The inside spread between the antlers is 19 1/8 inches. Antler mass was better than normal, totaling 40 1/8 inches, averaging five inches for each of the eight circumference measurements.

When the antlers from Mario's buck were green scored before the required 60-day drying period, they netted 168 4/8. They were measured more carefully when officially scored, yielding the slightly higher tally.

Regardless of the score, Mario is happy with his trophy buck. His odds of taking a whitetail of that caliber were obviously much higher than he thought. The same could be true for you.

The second nontypical point on the VanderMeulen Buck is at the base of the right antler.

Full mount of what most likely is Michigan's heaviest buck, which was bagged by Gavrill Fermanis in Oakland County during November of 1993.

Chapter 13

Michigan's Heaviest Buck

Most of the heaviest bucks on record for Michigan were bagged in the Upper Peninsula (U.P.). A chapter that discusses some of the state's heavy weight whitetails is in Book 1 of Great Michigan Deer Tales. One buck that should be in that chapter, but isn't, is a monster bagged with bow and arrow in Oakland County during November of 1993. The 12-pointer arrowed by Gavrill Fermanis from Northville (he lived in Dearborn Heights at the time he got his trophy buck) on November 11th that year is definitely one of Michigan's heaviest bucks, if not the heaviest, with a live weight exceeding 400 pounds.

That buck's typical antlers were also impressive. They are large enough to qualify for an alltime place in national records maintained by the Boone and Crockett Club, with a final net score of 170 2/8. Typical whitetail antlers have to measure a minimum of 170 to make that prestigious list.

However, the gross score more clearly reflects how large this buck's antlers really are. The rack grossed 182 3/8. There are 12 1/8 inches of deductions for nontypical points and lack of symmetry from one antler to the other. The rack has a typical 10-point frame, with a pair of nontyical tines on the right antler.

The nontypical points are 1 2/8 and 2 2/8 inches in length, contributing 3 4/8 inches in deductions. There are also some major differences in tine lengths from one antler to the other. The second tine on the right side is 8 7/8 inches long compared to 10 1/8 inches for the same tine on the left antler, a difference of 1 2/8 inches.

There's another 1 7/8 inches of deductions for the third point (9 6/8 versus 7 7/8) and 3 1/8 inches of difference between the lengths of the fourth points (5 3/8 compared to 8 4/8). Long beams that are similar in length helped contribute to the high score. The right antler is 28 7/8 inches long and the left is 29 4/8. Inside spread between the beams is 19 6/8 inches.

Bases of the beams are also heavy, measuring 5 6/8 inches on each side. All of the other circumference measurements on each side, with one exception, are between four and five inches. The exception is the last circumference on the left antler. The smallest circumference between the third and fourth points on that beam is 5 2/8 inches, which is exceptionally heavy that far out on the beam.

One of the most important things about Fermanis' trophy buck success is that little luck was involved. He earned the whitetail of a lifetime through experience, patience, persistence and skill. He's a serious bowhunter dedicated to spending as much time as possible in an effort to take a mature buck.

During the fall of 1993, for example, he hunted at least 23 days in October and 11 days of November before finally connecting on the buck he wanted. It was about 4:00 p.m. on November 11th when he scored. That's 34 days of deer hunting. Gavrill said he spent either a morning or evening in the field most days during the week. He hunted all day on Sundays.

The fact that the bowhunter knew the exceptional whitetail was in the area served as incentive to keep trying. Fermanis knew there were other good bucks in the area, too. He said he saw nine different bucks during the 1993 season.

Success during previous years also kept Gavrill motivated. He said he had been bowhunting for at least 15 years by 1993. During the three years prior to '93, he had been successful in taking one good buck annually. Fermanis said he had taken those bucks from the same stand where he got the booner, one during each of the preceding years. Interestingly, the bucks got progressively bigger and were taken a little bit later in the season each year. Gavrill's string of success started in 1990 with a 6-pointer. He got that deer on October 3rd.

Then in 1991, Fermanis bagged a 7-pointer on October 10th. He said that whitetail was an old animal because its teeth were badly worn and the antlers were probably shaped differently than when the deer was younger. One of the oldtimer's antlers was shaped like a shovel.

A buck with a perfect 8-point rack fell to one of Gavrill's arrows on October 15, 1992. He credits increased hunting time for the improvement in his harvest rate on bucks between 1990 and 1993. Prior to 1990, he wasn't spending as much time bowhunting as he had been since and he didn't take as many deer either.

"Prior to 1990, I only hunted a couple of days a week," he said. "I used to get frustrated because I didn't see anything and would just quit hunting. Now I know the more I hunt, the better my chances are of seeing deer."

Gavrill also commented that hunting seems to have gotten better since 1990 on the private property where he bowhunts. The parcel is undeveloped, but houses are being built in adjoining areas. Increased development nearby appears to be forcing more whitetails into the remaining habitat. The nine bucks he saw in the fall of 1993 are the most he had seen during any previous year, but he spent more time hunting, too.

Fermanis' stand was situated in a big oak tree in a field on a hill. He said there's a swamp 100 yards downhill from the stand. Woods surround the field and there's a thicket on at least one side. The platform was positioned 30 feet from the ground in the oak tree.

"I like to hunt high," he said. "It gives you a good view and you don't spook deer."

To help him blend in with his surroundings, Gavrill varies the camouflage clothes he wears to match his surroundings. When the leaves are still on the trees and there's a lot of green, he wears a green pattern. He changes to brown after leaves have dried and turned that color along with the grass in the field. He also owns a set of snow camo for times when that pattern is appropriate. A face mask and gloves are important items in helping Fermanis remain unseen while hunting. He doesn't use any scents because he believes they would attract attention to his location. He tries to remain as natural as possible, in terms of scent, while hunting, often washing with water and no soap.

Practice with his bow and arrows was a daily ritual with him. He used to shoot in his back yard every day after work for as much as two hours at a time. Back in 1993, Gavrill hunted with a Hoyt Fast Flite Bow set at 76 pounds, with 22 1/2-inch aluminum arrows. He used an old Bear brand release that he really likes. The broadheads he puts on his arrows for hunting are 125 grain Thunderheads.

Although Gavrill is a dedicated bowhunter, he started deer hunting with a centerfire rifle about 25 years before he got his trophy whitetail. He has also hunted with a muzzleloader. Most of his gun hunting is done "up north" where he has never had much luck getting a big buck. Most of the bucks bagged in that part of the state have been spikes and forkhorns.

He said he likes bowhunting much more than spending time afield with a firearm.

Archery equipment affords him more quiet time to enjoy the outdoors and he especially likes to be hunting during early October when vegetation is thick and leaves are on the trees. He also prefers bowhunting because the equipment increases the challenge involved in connecting as well as giving deer more of a chance of getting away.

"Bowhunting is my cup of tea," Fermanis commented. "I don't like guns as much for hunting because it doesn't give deer too much of a chance. If you see one, it's yours."

Not so with bow and arrow, as Gavrill found out during the first week of November in 1993. He saw a nice 10-pointer one day and decided to shoot it because it was the best buck he had within bow range since the season started. The whitetail was 25 yards away and walking when Fermanis drew and released.

As he released, he was aware of his bow arm moving upward a little bit. That movement was enough to send the arrow high, going over the buck's back. The deer jumped and ran after the shaft hit the ground. Gavrill guessed that animal's antlers might have scored in the 150s.

Fermanis said he first saw the B&C buck he got in '93 while bowhunting the previous year. The animal was too far away for a shot at the time. During March of 1993 he found one of the buck's shed antlers; the left beam. He said the shed only had five points and proved to be a little smaller than the antler that replaced it by the fall of 1993.

Gavrill saw the booner twice during the fall before the day he got it. He said he knew the deer had a nice rack, but he didn't realize how big the antlers really were. He said he figured they would score in the 150s like the 10-pointer he missed. The fact that the deer's body was so big, may have made his antlers appear smaller than they were.

Both times the 12-pointer was spotted were during the evening. One time the whitetail traveled to the right on a trail and the second time he walked to the left on the same runway. On one of those occasions, the buck was walking toward Fermanis' stand, but then changed directions for an unknown reason. The next time, the book buck joined two does that were feeding about 50 yards away.

The circumstances were different on the afternoon of November 11th, which was a clear, cold day. A group of does were involved this time, too, but they worked to Gavrill's advantage. At least one of them was in heat because there were two other bucks that were interested in them besides the 12-pointer. One of the bucks had 10 points and the other was an 8-pointer. Fermanis said he wasn't sure if the 10-point was the one he missed the week before.

The experienced bowhunter had only been in the stand about 10 minutes when the small herd of whitetails appeared. The 12-pointer was with the group of four does initially. Then the does left his company and walked in front of Fermanis' stand. At that point the smaller of the three bucks was in perfect position for a bow shot, but it was easy for Gavrill to pass him up with two larger whitetails in view.

The 10-pointer was the first buck to make a move toward the does and the 12-pointer soon followed in an effort to cut off his competition. The bigger buck's course brought him right under the prepared archer's perch no more than 12 to 15 yards away. The whitetail was so distracted, he had no idea a hunter was nearby. Fermanis' arrow entered the top of the deer's back between the shoulder blades.

The rest is history. Gavrill said he felt so honored, pleased and satisfied to take such a fine buck that the first thing he did when he walked up to the dead deer is to pick up its antlers and kiss it. Other hunters can certainly appreciate the emotions he was feeling at that moment.

The buck's antlers weren't the only thing about him worthy of note. His body was also huge. Gavrill said the whitetail had an actual live weight of 416 pounds. The deer was thought to be five or six years old.

Assuming the buck would have lost 15 percent of its live weight (62 pounds) during the process of being field dressed, the whitetail would have had a dressed weight of 354 pounds. That's the same weight recorded for what has been labeled as Michigan's heaviest whitetail, a 10-pointer that Albert Tippett shot in Ontonagon County during 1919. Based on that deer's actual dressed weight, the live weight of Tippett's buck was estimated at 425 pounds, but in reality, it could have been lighter.

In fact, there's an excellent chance that the Fermanis Buck weighed more than the Tippett Buck. Gavrill shot his whitetail during the beginning of the rut, before the deer had the opportunity to use up much of its fat reserves. Tippett shot his big-bodied whitetail on the last day of firearms season during a snow storm, toward the end of the rut, after the buck would have used up a lot of his fat reserves.

So there's a strong possibility that Gavrill bagged the heaviest buck on record for Michigan, especially in view of the fact that its live weight was recorded. And the deer's actual live weight would have been more than 416 pounds due to blood loss between the time the buck was shot and it was weighed. Of course, there's also the distinct possibility that the weights of the Fermanis and Tippett Bucks were close to the same since the estimated dressed weight of Gavrill's deer was the same as Tippett's buck. Gavrill had a full mount done of the outstanding whitetail he got in 1993.

Another bowhunter who has had excellent success on Oakland County's trophy bucks is Jerry Pennington from Oxford. One of the

Michigan's Heaviest Buck

chapters in Book 1 of <u>Great Michigan Deer Tales</u> is about some of the whitetails Jerry has tagged in the county, including a 10-pointer netting 174 7/8 that he got during late December of 1992. Another 10-point he got the year before that netted 169 5/8, is also covered.

The late Albert Tippett with the buck he shot in Ontonagon County on the last day of the 1919 season that was previously thought to be Michigan's heaviest buck. It had a dressed weight of 354 pounds.

The Tahquamenon Club in 1980 along the Tahquamenon River.

Ken Teysen in his role as chief cook in 1970.

Tom Alexander (left) enjoys a card game at camp during 1993.

Photos courtesy Ken Teysen

Chapter 14

50 Years of Deer Camp

The 1999 firearms deer season marked a special anniversary for 78-year-olds Ken Teysen and Tom Alexander from Mackinaw City. It was their 50th year as deer hunting buddies and joint owners of one of the U.P.'s oldest deer camps. The pair spent each of those years hunting whitetails from the camp and have plenty of fond memories of their time afield as well as many of the experiences associated with camp life.

The pair are also proud of carrying on the camp tradition, which has been in existence twice as long as they have owned it. Their camp is Luce County's Tahquamenon Club. It's located along the Tahquamenon River, three miles upstream from the big falls. Teysen and Alexander represent the third generation of hunters/owners.

The club was formed by a group of men from Saginaw around 1901, with William S. Linton serving as club president for over 25 years. Linton was Saginaw's Postmaster for a number of years and also served as mayor of the city besides being a state representative and congressman. Senator Harvey Penney was also a member of the camp during the early 1920s. Other members listed on the roster for 1923 were Fred Bearinger, J. W. Fordney, Ed Peters and Hiram Savage.

The present camp is actually at a different location than the original structure. The first camp was constructed five miles upstream from the falls on land owned by the Northwestern Lumber

101

and Veneer Company from Gladstone. In 1933, the lumber company requested that the camp be moved to its present location three miles from the falls. The company leased the club an acre of land to put the camp on for $10 per year. Forty-one acres that the camp is on was eventually purchased for $1,000.

A new camp was built on the site during 1933 at a cost of $619.19, including new beds and mattresses. Water was dipped from a nearby creek the first two years, but by 1935, a pump had been installed in the kitchen to allow easier access to the valuable liquid. A generator to power electric lights was purchased for $45 in 1937. A new camp stove was bought and installed prior to the 1941 season at a cost $23.50.

Due to the camp's remoteness, getting there during the early years was a major task. Members would travel by train from Saginaw to Newberry and then get to the camp in horse drawn wagons. The process would take days. As more camps were established along the river, a boat called the Betty B that was operated by Joe Beach and later by his son RJ, provided service to the camps.

The boat ran every other day and dropped hunters off at 15 to 20 camps that were along the river. The fee to be ferried to camp by the Betty B was $40.

Although boat service shortened the trip to the camp, it still took almost a full day to get from Mackinaw City to the hunting grounds. Soo Junction was the jumping off point for regular rail service. From there, members of the Tahquamenon Club took the narrow gauge Toonerville Trolley to the river. The boat trip was 20 to 25 miles.

The normal camp stay in those days was two weeks to a month. Club members took deer hunting seriously and they often got their share of whitetails. According to a history of the camp's first 50 years written by Ken Teysen, some of the best hunting occurred during the 1920s and early 30s.

"Game was plentiful. Few, if any, other camps were nearby and the taking of 12 deer by 14 hunters was a regular event. The favored method of hunting was to place men along various old tote roads and make drives."

A tattered black and white photograph of the camp game pole taken in 1933 shows a total of 17 deer hanging - nine bucks and eight does. That year duffle, groceries and other camp supplies were shipped from Saginaw on November 4th. Camp members headed north on the 10th.

It was the late 1940s when Ken and Tom became involved in the camp. They were both born and raised in Saginaw, but they didn't meet until they were out of the service after World War II ended and living in Mackinaw City. Ties to their home town and deer hunting drew them together at the camp.

Ken's father Harry had been a member of the Tahquamenon Club for 15 years when Ken was voted in during 1947. Tom's brothers Pete and Bob were members of the camp and in the normal progression of events, Tom joined, too. When the camp was put up for sale in 1949 by the aging owners, the Alexander Brothers and the Teysens bought it along with Bill Blackmer and Harvey Eno from Millington. The membership of Ed Swiss was also transferred from the old camp to the new.

The camp and land were purchased for $2,500 and an additional $175 was paid for the camp boat, which was essential to transport hunters and deer from one side of the river to the other. Both Ken and Tom knew the camp was special when they agreed to buy it. Over the 50 years they owned it, the home away from home has become even more special to the pair as it has played a prominent role in their lives.

"Deer hunting is the excuse we use to go there for an extended stay," they said, "but there's no other place we'd rather be. We always had such a good time there regardless of how the deer hunting was. We don't think we had any bad experiences at camp. We had all good experiences.

"We have a waiting list of people who want to join the camp. Right now we limit membership to seven people. Between members and their guests, we usually have 12 to 14 of us hunting out of camp. Half hunt one side of the river and half hunt the other side. We always used to get four to eight bucks between us, but deer numbers have been going down since the late 1980s.

"There were huge beech trees in the area when we started hunting out of camp. You could see well and there were beech nuts everywhere. Deer were like butterballs. You could pick your deer then.

"There's a lot of bear up there, too. They like the beech nuts as much as the deer. When it was legal to shoot bear during deer season, we shot at them, but I guess we had buck fever because most of those shots missed. Tom shot the only bear and it wasn't very big."

It was in 1958 when Tom shot the bear. That information is listed on a sheet of paper that summarizes hunting success out of the camp from 1951 through 1979. During those years, a total of 82 bucks were bagged, with 55 of them taken on the west side of the river and 27 from the east side. The camp average was 2.8 bucks per year.

Average hunting success was 27.9 percent for those years. The average number of days of hunting per buck was 22.7. And the average number of points on bucks bagged from the camp was 4.3.

The best year in terms of the number of bucks tagged was 1954 when seven were shot. Five tags were filled each of three years - 1951, 1952, and 1963. The three worst years when no deer were shot fell during the 1970s - 1970, 1972 and 1978.

Part of the camp tradition is for each hunter to put $2 in a kitty before opening day. The pot is split evenly between the person who gets the first buck for the season and the biggest buck.

Low camp membership as well as few deer contributed to poor success during the 70s. By the late 70s, there were only six members hunting out of the camp. The cost per hunter had risen to $101 per season then to use the camp instead of the more normal fee of $50.

Between the years 1951 and 1979, the buck with the biggest rack taken out of camp was an 18-pointer that Dave Swiss shot in 1971. A 12-pointer was shot during the 1973 season. The most successful member was Bill Blackmer, with 16 bucks to his credit. Ken was second in line with nine.

The river was a major landmark for hunters who spent time at the Tahquamenon Club, but they also blazed a couple of prominent trails to help guide them to and from their residence when afield. The Red Trail extended for two miles to the west of camp. The Green Trail was blazed to the south.

"While most hunters knew the territory quite well," Ken wrote, "the blazed trees were a most welcome sight to a tired hunter returning to camp some time after 4:30 p.m. when the light was failing and snow was falling. Since there were no roads or trails to follow and almost no other hunters present, except our own, it was like seeing a familiar face to hit the Red Trail and the path for home. Missing this guideline could mean a walk of four to five miles north to the big falls or even to Lake Superior.

"Losing one's way was not only possible, it actually happened to at least two of our most experienced woodsmen; both times at night in a blizzard. Fortunately, both found their way to a neighboring camp safely. Lost hunters were much more common prior to the mid-1950s.

Teysen said he got more bucks while walking than sitting, but stand hunting was responsible for his most successful day of deer hunting. It was opening day of firearms season and he was posted at first light when he heard brush breaking. He saw a set of rocking chair antlers when he looked in the direction of the sound and took three shots.

The big 8-pointer had a dressed weight of 198.5 pounds and it fell near his truck. Later that day, Ken went back to the same spot and fell asleep. Another 8-pointer that was 50 pounds lighter than the first one, was in view when he woke up and he also shot that one. Bill Blackmer bagged a pair of 8s that day, too.

Some of the big bucks got away. Ken once experienced what many deer hunters have nightmares about. He had a big 10-pointer looking at him and his rifle wouldn't fire. He didn't find out until later that he had a broken firing pin.

Antlerless deer also provided some memorable moments. On two occasions, Ken had does with fawns that were distracted, almost run him over. On one of those occasions, the fawn bumped into a sapling and fell down. The second time he was almost run over, the fawn came so close to Ken that he was able to reach out and touch it. He said it reacted like it had gotten an electric shock.

Tom prefers stand hunting and he normally takes a magazine with him to read while waiting for whitetails to appear. He earned the camp's "Reader's Digest Award" one fall for missing a big buck that showed up while he was reading. He saw the whitetail when he looked up from the page. Alexander was so surprised by the buck's presence and was concerned about getting a shot before it departed, that he wasn't as careful about his aim as he would have liked.

Tom also connected on a pair of 8-pointers one season, but he got them on successive days rather than the same one. He got one of the bucks while walking during the morning. The next afternoon, the second buck wandered by while he was posted.

Over the years, camp has become more accessible as new roads have been established in that country. In 1952 or '53, a new road was built from Newberry to the Upper Falls and Paradise. That road made it possible for the men to drive to within three miles of camp. They used a boat to get to camp from there.

New logging roads then made it possible to drive within a mile of camp. A one-wheeled cart called a deer buggy was then put into service to haul gear and supplies. The buggy also came in handy for transporting deer that members got.

The road got closer and closer to camp until it became possible to drive directly there. With the increased convenience of getting to camp, Ken and Tom now visit more often, making trips there at various times of year, not just deer season. However, deer season at camp still remains the highlight of their year.

Ken currently has a cabin of his own three to four miles upstream from the hunting camp. One year during October when he decided to take a walk from his cabin to the camp, he got turned around. Part of the problem was he got his glasses snagged on a tree while going through some thick brush and lost them. Fortunately, it was a moonlit night.

Teysen ended up at the Church Camp three to four miles downstream from his intended destination. He managed to get inside to find something to eat then rowed a boat that was there to the Tahquamenon Club. It was about midnight before he got home.

The camp itself has been modified over the years, a little at a time. Members usually have work bees three or four times a year to take care of camp projects. A well was put in to provide a clean water supply about 1985. A new outhouse made of cedar (a 2-seater), was installed more recently. The reason cedar was selected for the outhouse is porcupines don't chew on it.

Although Ken and Tom are still active in the camp, their sons are taking their places as serious deer hunters. Ken's son Greg got

Greg Teysen at camp buck pole in November 1980. (photo coutesy Ken Teysen)

a big 8-pointer one year that weighed over 200 pounds dressed and he bagged a 10-pointer another time. Greg won the "Marlin Perkins Award" one of those years when he saw a second buck that was smaller than the one he already had. He photographed the whitetail and then threw a stick at it to scare it away when it wouldn't leave.

"Just seeing deer now is fine with us," Ken and Tom told me. "We don't care if we kill anything anymore. We don't hunt as hard as we used to. It's just a privilege to be at camp. It helps us appreciate how good life is."

Ken has been "chief cook and bottle washer" at the camp for many years, a role he still enjoys. The job came naturally since he owned a restaurant in Mackinaw City for many years. Teysen was not only well qualified to do the cooking, he probably didn't have much competition for the duty.

How was the 1999 season at the Tahquamenon Club?

"As usual, we had a great time," Ken said. "We saw 30 does and maybe two or three bucks. We got one buck between 13 guys. It had six or seven points. Of course, getting a deer is not the reason we go!"

John Benedict with the B&C 10-point he arrowed on November 7, 2002. The impressive antlers net 180 2/8 and are tied for second place in state records among typical bow kills.

Chapter 15

Down To Earth Bowhunting Expert

John Benedict from Auburn Hills is one of Michigan's most successful bowhunters and he's a down to earth kind of guy in more ways than one. He's humble, religious, a serious deer hunter and he doesn't mind sharing what he's learned about whitetail hunting. But, most importantly for the purposes of this chapter, he's taken the majority of his many book bucks while hunting from the ground.

He has 27 deer in state records maintained by Commemorative Bucks of Michigan (CBM), all but two of which were collected with bow and arrow. Most years, he fills both of his Michigan buck tags with whitetails that qualify for CBM records. During recent years, the bucks he's bagged in the state with bow and arrow have been large enough to qualify for national archery records kept by the Pope and Young Club in addition to state records.

In the fall of 2004, John's first book buck from Michigan was taken with an arrow and his second was shot with a muzzleloader. Two of John's bow bucks from recent years, 2004 and 2002, have had antlers large enough to qualify for alltime listing in national records maintained by the Boone and Crockett as well as Pope and Young Clubs. Both of those deer had typical antlers. During the fall of 2003 he also collected a nontypical with antlers large enough to qualify for the honorable mention category in Boone and Crockett.

Besides the booners John has bagged in Michigan, he's taken another one in Alberta and he's also filled bow tags with impressive whitetails in Iowa and Ohio. His bowhunting success from the ground has been phenomenal. His best typical is a huge Michigan 10-pointer from Clinton County that grossed 184 and nets 180 2/8, tying it for second place among typical bow kills listed in state records. Benedict's bow-bagged buck is the highest scoring typical on record for Clinton County. He got it on November 7, 2002.

John's other 2002 buck tag went on a 12-pointer he got in Midland County during October. Those antlers net 130.

His best nontypical is another 12-point he tagged in Lenawee County during 1994 that nets 189 7/8. The 13-point nontypical with double drop tines that he got in Monroe County on October 1, 2003, came close to the same score - 188 2/8. One more 12-pointer he got with an arrow in Wayne County during 2000 is that county's number two nontypical that scores 171 5/8.

A total of 14 of the book deer Benedict has taken with archery equipment in Michigan also qualify for Pope and Young Records. Typical antlered bucks only have to measure 100 to qualify for CBM Records and the minimum is 125 for nontypicals. Pope and Young minimums for the same categories are 125 and 150. Boone and Crockett minimums for alltime listing are 170 for typicals and 195 for nontypicals. For honorable mention in B&C, typicals must measure at least 160 and nontypicals 185. B&C accepts bow kills as well as gun kills that meet their high standards.

The fact that the 27 whitetails John has in state records have come from 20 different counties illustrates that he does a lot of moving around. He doesn't have one or two honey holes that produce for him on a consistent basis. How is he able to be so consistently successful on book bucks? Read on to find out what he told me over the past several years.

"I have pretty much committed to myself that I'm only going to shoot Pope and Young deer," Benedict said. "If I don't get a deer, that's alright. I feel just as successful coming home with a picture rather than putting meat in the freezer. I've learned a lot by reading about deer in books and magazines from people who are hunters, researchers and photographers.

"I don't have any real secrets," John continued. "I go look for the type of deer I'm after. I already know where there are a couple of dandies for next year (2003). I spend as much time hunting for permission as I do hunting for deer.

"A lot of people give up too easily when trying to get permission to hunt private land. If one person says no when they ask for permission to hunt, they get discouraged rather than asking the neighbor. I always ask the neighbor. And if I get permission to hunt from the neighbor, I go back to the person who said, 'No,' and tell them if they see me or my vehicle around, I'm not trying to sneak on their property, I got permission to hunt from their neighbor.

"They will sometimes give me permission to hunt then, too. If they don't, I ask if it's okay to follow after a deer on their property that I shoot on their neighbor's land.

"I never ask for permission to hunt," John emphasized. "I ask to bowhunt. If I encounter a skeptic, I give them a copy of my resume. I used to wear my military uniform, with my medals shined up, when seeking permission to try for a buck on private property.

"If I hear a report about a big deer, I always follow up on it. Rather than assume it's a false report or some one is exaggerating, I try to find out as much as I can about where the deer was seen. Then I refer to Platt Books to find out who owns the land and try to get permission to hunt. Once I have permission to hunt, I get aerial photos and topo maps of the area. I also refer to county maps.

"If I see a big buck while driving, I don't drive on by like most people do," Benedict commented. "I pull over and figure out exactly where I am, so I can find the place on maps. Then I try to get permission to hunt.

"One of the bucks I hope to get in the future is in Monroe County," John explained. "I was on my way to Tennessee on a business trip with my wife and I saw this buck in a field along a major highway. I've obtained permission to hunt the property where I think I've got the best chance of getting him. Just last weekend (early March), I prepared a spot to ambush him and blocked a fence crossing 60 yards away, so he's more likely to use one that's 30 yards from where I will be waiting."

John did, indeed, get that buck he was after in Monroe County on opening day of the 2003 bow season. It was the 13-pointer netting 188 2/8 with double drop tines mentioned earlier. He probably could have gotten the deer during 2002, but it had a couple of broken tines then, including one of the drop tines, so he decided to leave it alone until 2003.

Someone else could have easily gotten the whitetail in the meantime. Fortunately for John, no one did. Here are the particulars behind the hunt for that buck. It was mid-December of 2001 when he saw the buck from a highway.

"I noticed a trio of deer in the middle of a field that bordered the road on our left," Benedict related. "The one closest to the highway was sporting a giant set of antlers. He was at least a foot taller at the shoulders than his companions, and had a well proportioned nontypical rack. It looked like he had 10 typical points and five-inch drop tines off each beam.

"My heart accelerated and my car decelerated as I groped for the binoculars. By the time I could stop safely I would be too far down the road to glass them, so I let discretion outweigh valor and resumed speed. A casual observer would have thought that the encounter had not made much of an impression, but my mind was working overtime. I mentally recorded the closest mile marker and was planning my strategy for getting landowner permission to hunt the local farms."

By May of 2002, John had permission to hunt close to 100 acres. He then visited some of the parcels to locate the best places to hunt and set up ground blinds in strategic locations that he identified. His preseason preparations were complete by June 1.

His first hunt for the drop tine buck was on October 10, 2002. The weather was still warm and hornets had constructed a nest in the blind he wanted to hunt from. The stinging insects drove him from the spot. That left him little choice other than to hunt that evening from his backup spot.

"I hadn't been settled in for more than 30 minutes when six deer strolled into the field," Benedict explained. "They weren't any more than 100 yards away. Three were bucks, and one of them was big bodied, dominant and hostile. He chased anything that came within ten yards, spending a lot of time pawing the ground and rubbing his antlers on saplings and shrubs in the field.

"The big boy was a nontypical with more than 12 points. He had

10 typical tines, two drop tines and a few stickers here and there. I thought the drops were at least six inches long at first, but when he turned and looked my way, I could see that one side was broken off at about two inches. He had also broken off part of a G3 tine on one side."

That's when John decided he didn't want to take the deer with a damaged rack. He didn't return to his hunting spot in Monroe County until March of 2003. He got rid of the hornet's nest from his best blind, made some better shooting lanes and tried to encourage deer traffic near the blind. That's when he plugged a hole in a fence 60 yards away that deer had been using, so whitetails would be more likely to use a break in the fence much closer to the blind.

Benedict visited the spot one more time before opening day to make sure the hornets weren't back, to retrim shooting lanes and to clear a path to approach the blind on, so he could do it quietly. He did those things during late June. On October 1, 2003, John was in that blind before first light. It was a cool day, with rain in the forecast; conditions that would be expected to encourage deer activity and eliminate concerns about biting insects.

John Benedict with the antlers and skull of the double drop tine buck scoring 188 2/8 that he got in Monroe county October 1, 2003. He does European mounts like this of many of his deer.

"At first light, a herd of does came through the fence and wandered into the field on a trail that passed within 10 yards of my blind," John wrote. "A half hour later, a 5-pointer and an 8-pointer that would score close to 100 inches followed the same route. Then about 10:30, three small bucks materialized in the middle of the nearest field.

"A while later, a doe with a spotted fawn jumped the fence and either saw me or caught my scent. All through a 10-minute pounding downpour she bobbed her head and stomped her foot at me. When the rain stopped, she wandered off without spooking or snorting.

"It was close to noon and I was sneaking a drink of bottled water from my drenched pack," Benedict continued, "when movement caught my eye. There was a deer paralleling the fence, headed toward the break. He stopped, lifted his head to scan the field, and my heart jumped into my throat. It was the buck I had been dreaming about for months.

"Luckily I didn't choke on the water, but I had to exchange the bottle for my bow before he jumped the fence and got too close for the required movement. He appeared to be alone, but checked his back trail a couple of times before starting to move. When he put his head down and out of sight behind the brush along the fence, I got rid of the bottle and grabbed my bow. "It took a good ten minutes for the buck to decide to jump the fence, but he finally did and moved along the same route as all the deer before him. Broadside, quartering away at between ten and fifteen yards, I released the arrow and watched it disappear into his rib cage. Before he went out of sight across the field, I could see that he was staggering."

Soon after John arrowed the trophy buck, he saw another big deer coming and he nocked an arrow in case it was a second book animal. However, it proved to be a huge doe that was followed by two more.

As you can see from the above example, Benedict does a lot of planning and preparation to put him in position to score on book bucks and anyone else can do the same thing. Scouting is a year-round activity for John. Even when he's turkey hunting, looking for morels or fishing, he's always got his eyes and ears open for anything that can contribute to his deer hunting success. He's always got a camera with him, too, so he can photograph any deer he happens to see while afield.

The Boone and Crockett 10-point he got during 2002, for example, he first saw during 1999 and managed to take some photographs of it. The whitetail was on property his nephew owns. John had misplaced a bleat call while hunting the property, so he went back to look for it. He spotted the 10-pointer bedded and managed to snap two photos of it laying down. Based on the size of the deer's body, Benedict thought the buck was 2 1/2 years old at the time.

Over the years that followed, John came to the conclusion that the buck spent most of its time elsewhere, but was always on his nephew's property during the first week of November. Benedict always takes a week off of work during November to bowhunt for deer and it's usually the first week of the month. Hunts out of state prevented John from connecting on the buck during 2000 and 2001, but his nephew saw the deer. Sign left by the whitetail also confirmed it was still around.

The veteran bowhunter concentrated on connecting on the trophy animal in 2002. John went home to vote on Tuesday, November 5th, and a neighbor spotted the buck that day. On the evening of November 6th, when it was too dark to shoot without a lighted sight pin, Benedict got a glimpse of the buck he was after. That sighting gave him the incentive he needed to know the buck was still in the area and John was back for another try on November 7th. He was hunting from a ground blind composed of natural cover.

"I had a perfect blind in a little woods," John said. "The three best deer trails that went through that woods were all within bow range. The wind was wrong for the blind until 4:30 p.m. I monitor a web site that gives the hourly wind direction and I knew the wind was supposed to change. Even though I wear a Scent-Lok Suit and think it helps reduce the chances of deer smelling me, I still pay careful attention to the wind.

"I moved back into the blind after the wind changed. It was getting dusky when he came down a fenceline. He was uphill from me, so he was silhouetted against the sky. When I saw his antlers silhouetted, I knew he was an exceptional buck.

"I grunted with my mouth to stop him when he was 30 yards away and broadside. When I released the arrow, I heard a crack like you broke a limb over your knee. I thought the arrow might have hit a sapling and deflected, but I could tell by his reaction that he was hit. The arrow actually hit a rib that made that cracking sound."

The ground was covered with yellow leaves speckled with red and even with a flashlight, John figured he would have a hard time finding blood, so he decided to return in the morning to recover the buck. As it turned out, there wasn't a lot of blood to find. Benedict's aluminum arrow tipped with a 3-blade Wasp Broadhead had gone through the top of both lungs. The high hit resulted in a sparse blood trail.

The whitetail had also gone farther than expected. The mature buck had gone through a stand of pine trees and into a woods where it bedded temporarily and then attempted to jump a fence. It was 11 a.m. when John found the buck, much to his relief, about a quarter mile from where he shot it. He said it appeared as though the deer died in midair while jumping the fence.

At the time John recovered the whitetail, he thought the antlers might be big enough for a state record bow kill. They ended up scoring short of that, but not by much. With a net score of 180 2/8, 1 5/8 inches short of the current record, that 10-pointer is tied for second place among typical bow kills with an 11-pointer Rock Vore arrowed in Oakland County during 1994. The story about the hunt on which Vore got his buck is in Book 3 of Great Michigan Deer Tales.

One year, Benedict was monitoring a perfect 12-pointer near Pinckney that he was confident had a rack that would qualify as a state record. Unfortunately, that buck suddenly disappeared without a trace. John suspects the deer may have been taken by a poacher.

"There have been more big deer that I was scouting killed by poachers than I would like to think about," Benedict commented. "That's the biggest disappointment about Michigan hunting."

He's also seen excellent deer habitat lost to development. After the potential state record 12-pointer disappeared, the woods it used to live in were eliminated. A housing development now occupies the ground where that buck, and others before it, used to live.

Down to Earth Bowhunting Expert

John has shot all of his book bucks from the ground. He fell 15 feet from a tree in 1981 and that soured him on hunting above the ground. He was using a limb as a step to climb down when it broke under his weight. Fortunately, he wasn't seriously hurt.

"I ruined my bow and scared myself to death," he commented about the fall. "I still had my bow in my hands because I was maneuvering into position to lower it when I fell. I landed on my bow, which was a Bear Grizzly recurve, and I twisted a limb, ruining it.

"If I don't have any other choice, I will still go in a tree. I simply prefer not to. I enjoy hunting from the ground. I've got a knack for

Photo courtesy John Benedict

John at full draw from one of the natural blinds he has been successful from. This spot is in Macomb County. John got a 10-pointer here that netted 126 5/8.

it. I always use natural cover to make blinds. I not only cut shooting lanes, I cut approach lanes, so I can get in position without making noise. I do this months ahead of time."

John has been deer hunting for 46 years and bowhunting for 40 years. The last time he seriously hunted whitetails with a firearm was 1997 or '98, until the 2004 muzzleloader season. When he hadn't filled his second buck tag with bow and arrow, he decided to hunt with a .50 caliber Knight muzzleloader. He shot a 12-pointer (10-point typical frame with two stickers) with the front loader in Jackson County at 1:15 p.m. on December 17th and the antlers netted 146 3/8.

"I have had such good luck with a bow that I'm usually tagged out by the time gun season opens," Benedict said, "or I have a big deer located in a bow only area. What's so appealing about bowhunting is the fact I see more game and I like the fact deer are close enough to see what they are all about before you can shoot."

John has been bowhunting with a compound bow since 1988.

"I wrestled in college and separated a shoulder," he said. "I could draw a recurve, but had a hard time holding it at full draw. In 1988 I borrowed my son's compound. I had such good luck with it, I went out and bought one for myself."

Benedict bought a Hoyt Spectra Eclipse bow with a 70 pound pull and 65 percent letoff in 1989 and he's used it ever since. The bow is equipped with a crosshair type sight that he uses as a range finder as well as to aim. John said he has to use a sight with a range finder because he's blind in his left eye.

He lost sight in the eye when he went down in a helicopter in Viet Nam. His ribs also separated from his sternum during the crash, but that injury healed within a year.

Two of the crosshairs on his bow sight are set as aiming points for 15 and 30 yards. The third crosshairs is the rangefinder.

John uses a string release to shoot his bow. It's a caliper type release with a wrist strap.

To sum up what is responsible for his bowhunting success, Benedict often tells people it's by following the three Ps and Rs. The three Ps are persistence, patience and prayer. The three Rs are restraint (passing up small bucks), readiness (practice and being prepared for a shot when the time comes) and repoire (being in touch with what's going on around you and having an idea what might happen next).

He credits the five years he spent in Germany in the military for helping him learn restraint. While there, he got a hunting license on his own and it took 10 months of study to get it. He had to pass three tests - written, oral and one in the field - to get the license. Part of the requirements were the ability to judge deer on the hoof.

The reason for that is during prerut hunts, large mature breeding stock have to be passed up. Bucks that aren't desirable breeding stock are removed from herds then. When John returned to the states, he did a lot of reading and studying videos to help him learn how to field judge whitetails. He passes up about 20 bucks a year that don't meet his standards as shooters.

Of the 77 bucks Benedict had taken through 2004, 53 were taken with bow and arrow. Twenty-one of them were shot during the prerut period - before the end of October. He's taken four bucks on opening day of bow season, but three of them are of Pope and Young caliber.

Thirty-six of his bucks have been taken during the rut, which is late October and early November. And John has bagged 23 bucks after November 15. All but six of those were shot during December (postrut).

When asked if he ever gets nervous when preparing for a shot at a big buck, he responded like a true combat veteran: "There's no reason to get nervous. They don't shoot back."

Although his answer was spoken partly in jest, there's a lot of truth in those words. Hunters who haven't been in combat certainly can't appreciate what it feels like to be in a life or death situation on a daily basis. The emotions generated by shooting at the world's largest whitetail are insignificant compared to what it must feel like to battle for your life. It certainly puts a different perspective on deer hunting.

John obviously manages to get the job done when presented with a bow shot at trophy bucks because he's done it over and over again. Here's what else he had to say on the subject:

"I'm a calm natured person; not the kind of person that tends to panic. I will envision the target, trying to concentrate on the shot rather than lock in on the whole deer. The more deer you see and watch, the more comfortable you get. That's probably part of it."

One of his December bucks is the 12-point nontypical from Lenawee County scoring 189 7/8. He calls that one the heart attack buck. A father of a friend of John's wounded the deer during gun season and immediately suffered a heart attack. The friend told Benedict about the deer and asked him if he would try to get it.

John spent a lot of time looking for the buck and finally jumped it out of a five acre swamp on the property. He said the buck was living in the swamp and once he figured that out it wasn't too difficult to determine what trail the deer would most likely be using and that's where he got the whitetail.

When bowhunting for deer, John carries two calls that most other hunters don't. One is a squirrel call and the other is a snort call made by Lohman. When ever Benedict is moving through the woods, he tries to move like an animal would. He blows the squirrel call to better create an illusion that the sounds he makes are coming from a squirrel and not a human.

"When a deer snorts at me, I will snort back at it. If you snort back at them and draw it out, it will stop them. Sometimes their curiosity will get the best of them and they will come back. Most of the time they don't."

The second year John used a snort call it helped him collect a 140-class 9-pointer with a 24-inch spread near Lapeer.

"It was dark as I was going into this spot in the morning when the buck snorted at me and I snorted back. About 10 a.m. he came back. He came in from the downwind side like he was trying to smell me. I was on the crest of a little rise where the wind swirls. I shot him before he smelled me."

The B&C buck John got with archery equipment during 2004 is an exceptional 10-point that he got in Eaton County on November 1. The antlers from that buck grossed 175 4/8 and netted 171. That rack is the highest scoring typical known taken in Michigan for the year, according to CBM.

John is one of only two bowhunters who have a pair of bucks with antlers large enough to qualify for B&C's alltime listing in CBM records. Jerry Pennington from Oxford was the first to accomplish the feat. In 2002, he bow-bagged a 26-point nontypical that nets 217 6/8 in Oakland County. During the 1992 bow season, he arrowed a 10-point typical in the same county that nets 174 7/8.

What's even more amazing about John's 2004 Michigan season besides the fact that he tagged two book bucks, one of which is of B&C proportions, is that the day before he got the first one in Eaton County, he missed another whitetail with a rack close to the caliber of the one he got.

Benedict's most recent booner was taken on property where he shot his second buck ever 40 years earlier. The 3-pointer was brought down with a slug from a borrowed .410 shotgun. At the time, the property consisted of 350 acres, but the parcel owned by relatives of a friend had been downsized to 40 acres by the time John scouted a 25-acre woodlot on the parcel during the spring of 2004.

The scouting mission paid off in the form of the largest set of sheds John had ever found in Michigan. Those sheds prompted him to plan on hunting the property during the fall of 2004. He returned to the spot during early summer to prepare a pair of ground blinds.

"I picked out one spot in the northeast corner of the woods that overlooked a cornfield," John wrote, "and another location deeper in the woods along a main trail from the corn to the bedding area. The first spot was at the intersection of a ridge that ran through the field and the woodline. I constructed a couple of rudimentary ground blinds using branches and debris from recent windstorms and cut a few shooting lanes.

"The area where the ridge intersected the woods seemed to be the most likely point for a buck to enter the field. A few steps into the field would put him in the only spot that gave an unobstructed view of the entire field. So my plan was to use this blind unless the wind prevented me."

Benedict was in that blind on Halloween evening.

"My blind was intact and it worked as planned. A shooter nontypical came in as the light was fading and I took the shot when he was broadside at about 30 yards. In low light, my one-eyed view is without much depth perception. My arrow struck a young ash tree dead center that I hadn't noticed and the buck trotted into the field with his tail at half mast. He didn't like the commotion, but he never really figured out what happened."

It was that whitetail that had dropped the sheds that John found in the spring. He returned to the same blind by first light the following day, hoping for another chance at the buck. He saw a trio of does headed for the cut cornfield around daylight. It was almost 8:30 when he heard the sound of a buck grunting and deer running.

The sounds were coming from the field. The deer that made them were out of sight, over the ridge. It didn't take long for a doe to crest the ridge at a run, with a beautiful buck 10 feet behind her. The buck was a different one than John had seen the evening before, but it was also a shooter. The doe ran straight for the woods and entered the cover about 50 yards from where Benedict was waiting.

"The buck came to a screeching halt at the edge of the woods and stood there panting," John wrote. "Then he turned away from me and started walking along the edge of the field. I tried a soft grunt call and got no response. As he crested the ridge, headed back out into the field, I tried a bleat call. He still was not interested."

After the buck was out of sight, John tried rattling combined with grunt calls. After a half hour with no action, he was getting ready to do more calling when the same buck chased another doe into the woods and followed the same route back to the field.

"This time, when the buck went out of sight over the ridge I left my blind and headed down the woodline to find a closer seat for the next act," John continued. "I found where the does were entering the woods. A tree had recently fallen over the fence, taking down several feet of barrier, and there was already a well worn path. There was no real cover, so I found the closest tree big enough to hide behind and did a rattle/grunt sequence while clearing the leaves and debris away from where I needed to have some mobility if he showed up again."

About 45 minutes later, the buck came walking over the ridge by himself.

"He covered the distance from the top of the ridge to my kill zone without stopping or changing his pace," John explained. "He passed my tree at about 10 yards and I let him go another five yards before I did a bleat to stop him. When he looked at me, the arrow was already in flight. When the arrow hit, he did a 90 degree turn and was out of

Photo courtesy John Benedict

John with the Boone and Crockett 10-point he got in Eaton County on November 1, 2004 after missing a buck with antlers just as big the day before.

sight headed out the west side of the woodlot in seconds."

John said he waited a half hour to savor what he had accomplished as well as to let his heart rate return to normal. Once he started following the whitetail, it crossed onto property he didn't have permission to hunt, so he contacted the neighboring land owner and was able to get the okay to continue after the deer. Benedict found the B&C buck in a thick patch of brush in the middle of a harvested bean field.

The trophy whitetail had a dressed weight of 211 pounds and was aged at 5 1/2. The farmer who owned the land on which the buck died had seen the deer, but John didn't find that out until seeking permission to follow it onto the farmer's property. The farmer helped John retrieve the deer with his tractor.

The web address that John refers to for current weather information is http://asp.usatoday.com/weather/cityforecast.aspx?LocationID=USMI004. He obtains maps from http://terraserver.homeadvisor.msn.com/default.aspx?w=2.

John has written more than 50 stories about his hunts. He's thinking of publishing them in book form some time in the future. If he does, you can learn more about how he consistently scores on Michigan's book bucks.

The author applies the information he learns from interviewing Michigan's most successful deer hunters to his hunting and you can do the same. This is Richard P. Smith with a 10-pointer in got during November of 2003 that had a gross score of 153 1/8 at the time it was taken.

Author

Richard P. Smith is an award winning outdoor writer and photographer living in Marquette, Michigan with his wife and business partner Lucy. He is a nationally recognized writer, photographer and speaker who has written 21 books and thousands of magazine articles. He is one of only two people in Michigan who have qualified for a Commemorative Bucks of Michigan (CBM) Grand Slam, which includes a deer, bear, elk and turkey that are all entered in state records maintained by CBM.

His best whitetail is a Saskatchewan 10-pointer he got in 1999 that qualified for honorable mention in Boone and Crockett Records with a net score of 163 7/8. Prior to that, he bagged a nontypical 12-pointer with a 9-inch drop tine from the same area that netted 165 3/8. His best Michigan buck is a typical 11-pointer he shot on public land in the Upper Peninsula (U.P.) that nets 148 4/8. He's taken a number of other bucks that score in the 140s.

A Saskatchewan black bear he bagged with a Knight muzzleloader during the spring of 2002 is the second highest scoring bruin in national muzzleloading records with a skull that measured 21 14/16. It's also in alltime Boone and Crockett Records. The following spring, he collected another trophy bruin that qualified for honorable mention in Boone and Crockett Records, with a skull scoring 20 2/16. Richard has four trophy bruins in Pope and Young Records that he got with bow and arrow and he also took a book bear with a muzzleloader in Michigan. One of Smith's latest books, Stand Hunting For Whitetails, was published by Stackpole Books during 2004. Stackpole also published another of the author's popular books - the 3rd edition of Deer Hunting - in 2003.

Smith is a Field Editor for Bear Hunting Magazine and Michigan Hooks & Bullets. He's the editor for Bear Facts, a quarterly newsletter published by the Michigan Bear Hunters Association. He writes for Woods-N-Water News, Michigan Sportsman Magazine and the Porcupine Press on a regular basis. His writing and photography have been published in national magazines including Deer & Deer Hunting, North American Whitetail, Buckmasters, Outdoor Life, American Hunter, Bowhunter and National Wildlife.

The author is a recognized expert on whitetail deer and black bear behavior and biology as well as hunting these species of big game. He has hunted deer and bear extensively in Michigan and throughout North America for 40 years.

Books by Richard P. Smith

Great Michigan Deer Tales, Book 4 - Whopper whitetails bagged in each region of the state are covered. Every chapter has at least one important lesson and some of them are loaded with important information for hunters. Read new information about the Rompola Buck, including a photo of the huge typical when it was alive. Find out about a World Record 8-Point bagged in Michigan. (128 pages)
Price: $16.50 postpaid; Book Sets - 2 for $28; 3 for $40; **4 for $50**

Great Michigan Deer Tales, Book 3 - This book contains what might be the state's best deer tale ever about North America's best buck ever taken by a one-of-a-kind whitetail hunter. Two chapters are devoted to unraveling the mystery behind a 12-pointer scoring more than the current world record that Mitch Rompola shot with bow and arrow during 1998. Other chapters are devoted to a hunt shared by a father and son on which the year's biggest buck was bagged, a 14-year-old whose first deer was a booner, a woman who bagged a state record whitetail with the help of her husband, a bowhunter who collected a world class buck on his first day of hunting, one of the state's most successful senior citizens and much, much more. (128 pages; 47 photos)
Price: $16.50 postpaid; Book Sets - 2 for $28; 3 for $40; **4 for $50**

Great Michigan Deer Tales, Book 2 - More Great Deer Tales. Read about the current state record typical taken in Jackson County during 1996. Find out about the biggest bucks bagged by women in the state. Learn about trophy bucks with locked antlers. Read about a trophy rack recovered after almost 40 years and the end of a 70-year mystery surrounding a B&C nontypical. (128 pages; 46 photos)
Price: $16.50 postpaid; Book Sets - 2 for $28; 3 for $40; **4 for $50**

Great Michigan Deer Tales, Book 1 - Learn How, Where and When some of the state's Biggest Bucks were bagged, including a Boone & Crockett bow kill taken in 1985 by Mitch Rompola from Traverse City. Read about whitetails with the largest ANTLERS as well as those that were the HEAVIEST and OLDEST. If you are interested in bagging a BOOK BUCK in Michigan, studying this collection of success stories will help make it happen. There's no better way to learn than from those who have already accomplished the feat. (128 pages; 40 photos)
Price: $15.50 postpaid; Book Sets - 2 for $28; 3 for $40; **4 for $50**

Tracking Wounded Deer - 2nd Edition - Learn how to recover all of the deer you shoot by reading blood sign, tracking after dark and in the snow and using a string tracker. Decide when to begin tracking, determine type of hit and distinguish between tracks of wounded and healthy deer. This book is must reading for bowhunters since trailing arrowed deer is part of every successful hunt. Eight pages of color photos show blood and hair sign. (160 pages; 72 photos)
Price: $19.50 postpaid

Stand Hunting for Whitetails (Revised) - Detailed coverage of the tricks of the trade for hunting from ground-based stands as well as tree stands. Learn the best places to hunt, most productive times, dressing for - 20 F, how to hunt safely above the ground and how to avoid being detected by deer from ground and elevated stands. Read about Boone and Crockett bucks and a hunt with baseball great Wade Boggs. Stand hunting is the most popular and effective whitetail hunting method. Learn how to do it more effectively! (256 pages; 181 photos)
Price: $18.50 postpaid

Deer Hunting - 3rd Edition - This best selling book was so popular it was updated in 2003 to include even more information and photographs, making it one of the most comprehensive books in print on the subject. Learn all you need to know to successfully hunt whitetails and mule deer. There are bonus chapters on deer biology, diseases and management, hunting ethics and more. For beginners or experienced veterans like the author. (325 pages; 139 photos)
Price: $20.00 postpaid

Animal Tracks & Signs Of North America - It's the first guide book including actual photos of wildlife tracks and sign rather than sketches. Bonus chapters cover aging tracks, tracking wildlife and much more. (271 pages; 200 photos)
Price: $20 postpaid.

Understanding Michigan Black Bear - 2nd Edition - Learn all about black bears; their habits, life history, behavior and how to avoid problems from them when in bear country. One of the chapters is a history of bear attacks. The text provides valuable insights into bear research and management. There's also detailed coverage of how an anti-hunting referendum was defeated. (256 pages; 126 photos)
Price: $19.50 postpaid

www.RichardPSmith.com

Book Order Form

Quantity		Price
_____	Great Michigan Deer Tales-Book 4 ($16.50)	_____
_____	Great Michigan Deer Tales-Book 3 ($16.50)	_____
_____	Great Michigan Deer Tales-Book 2 ($16.50)	_____
_____	Great Michigan Deer Tales-Book 1 ($15.50)	_____
_____	Deer Tales Sets - 2 for $28; 3 for $40; 4 for $50 Please specify which books sent to the same address. Save $15 on the complete set.	_____
_____	Tracking Wounded Deer ($19.50)	_____
_____	Stand Hunting for Whitetails ($18.50)	_____
_____	Deer Hunting - 3rd Edition ($20)	_____
_____	Animal Tracks & Signs of N.A. ($20)	_____
_____	Understanding Michigan Black Bear ($19.50)	_____
	Total Payment Enclosed	$ _____

Name_____

Address _____

City_____State_____Zip_____

Please remit by MasterCard, Visa, check or money order.
Circle card type:

MC/Visa#_____Expiration Date_____

Signature_____ Phone#_____

Please send US funds. Canadian orders add $1/book(parcel post) or $3/ book(air mail).
Prices include postage and handling. Make checks payable to:

Smith Publications
814 Clark St.
Marquette, MI 49855
www.RichardPSmith.com